Becoming the Compassion Buddha

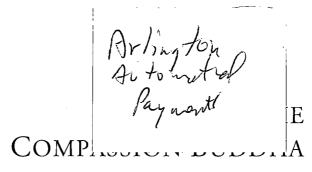

COMP~~ASSION BUDD~~A

TANTRIC MAHAMUDRA FOR EVERYDAY LIFE

A COMMENTARY ON THE GURU YOGA PRACTICE CALLED

The Inseparability of the Spiritual Master and Avalokiteshvara:
A Source of All Powerful Attainments,

Written by His Holiness the Dalai Lama at the Age of Nineteen

Lama Thubten Yeshe

Foreword by Geshe Lhundub Sopa

Edited by Robina Courtin

WISDOM·PUBLICATIONS • BOSTON

Wisdom Publications
199 Elm Street
Somerville MA 02144 USA
www.wisdompubs.org

*The Inseparability of the Spiritual Master and Avalokiteshvara: A Source of All Power-
ful Attainments* has been adapted from the translation by Sharpa Tulku and Brian
Beresford that appears in *Aryasura's Aspiration,* and is reprinted here with permission
from the publisher, The Library of Tibetan Works and Archives, Dharamsala, India.

Library of Congress Cataloging in Publication Data
Thubten Yeshe, 1935–1984
      Becoming the compassion Buddha : Tantric Mahamudra for everyday life : a
   commentary on the Guru Yoga practice called the Inseparability of the spiritual
   master and Avalokiteshvara : a source of all powerful attainments / by Lama
   Thubten Yeshe ; foreword by Geshe Lhundub Sopa ; edited by Robina Courtin.
         p.   cm.
      Includes index.
      ISBN 0-86171-343-5 (pbk. : alk. paper)
      1. Guru worship (Rite)—Buddhism. 2. Avalokiteśvara (Buddhist deity)—
   Cult. 3. Bstan-'dzin-rgya-mtsho, Dalai Lama XIV, 1935– Bla ma daṅ Spyan-ras-
   gzigs dbyer med kyi rnal 'byor dṅos grub kun 'byuṅ. 4. Mahāmudrā (Tantric rite)
   I. Courtin, Robina. II. Title.
      BQ7699.G87T594 2003
      294.3'444—dc21   2003002413

First Printing
07 06 05 04 03
 5   4   3   2   1

Designed by Gopa and Ted2
Line drawing on page 20 by Andy Weber

Printed in Canada

Contents

Foreword

IN THIS BOOK, Lama Yeshe gives a commentary on a practice composed by His Holiness the Dalai Lama called *The Inseparability of the Spiritual Master and Avalokiteshvara: A Source of All Powerful Attainments.* This commentary provides a detailed explanation of a special type of guru yoga practice, in which the deity is visualized not in the usual form of the deity or *yidam*, but in the form of one's actual guru.

We Tibetans consider His Holiness the Dalai Lama to be the manifestation of Avalokiteshvara. Therefore, it is much easier to see the guru, His Holiness the Dalai Lama, as inseparable from the yidam, Avalokiteshvara, and to envision Avalokiteshvara in the form of His Holiness the Dalai Lama. This commentary will be of great benefit to whoever engages in the Avalokiteshvara guru yoga practice written by His Holiness himself.

Lama Yeshe was one of my students, who studied all the philosophical topics and who later became tutor and guru of Lama Zopa Rinpoche. Lama Yeshe established Buddhist centers almost everywhere in the world, successfully, and those centers continue to develop and to train students who are great followers of the Dharma.

This book is a valuable contribution, and will be greatly beneficial to those who practice according to its instructions.

Geshe Lhundub Sopa
Deer Park Buddhist Center
Oregon, Wisconsin

Publisher's Acknowledgment

The Publisher gratefully acknowledges the generous help of the
Hershey Family Foundation in sponsoring the publication of this book.

Editor's Preface

LAMA THUBTEN YESHE gave these teachings at Chenrezig Institute in tropical Queensland, Australia, July 5–16, 1976, during his third visit to Australia. Set in 160 acres of hills inland from the Sunshine Coast, 100 kilometers north of the city of Brisbane, Chenrezig Institute was the first Dharma center of Lama Yeshe's in the West. The land was offered by some of his students at the end of the first course given by Lama in Australia, in September 1974, and the center was built during the following year.

Seventy people listened to the teachings and participated in the retreat that encompassed them and continued afterward. These teachings were preceded by a month-long course on the path to enlightenment *(lamrim)*, taught by Kyabje Thubten Zopa Rinpoche; such lamrim teachings are classically a prerequisite for hearing tantric teachings.

These teachings are a commentary on a short practice called *The Inseparability of the Spiritual Master and Avalokiteshvara: A Source of All Powerful Attainments*. Avalokiteshvara, Chenrezig in Tibetan, is the buddha of compassion. This practice was written by His Holiness the Fourteenth Dalai Lama when he was nineteen years old (at the repeated requests of a disciple). It is a guru yoga practice in which the buddha to be visualized is in the aspect of the guru (in Tibetan, *lama*) in his usual form, in this case His Holiness the Dalai Lama. This practice belongs to the first of the four levels of tantric practice called *kriya*, or action, tantra.

As practiced in tantra, the most advanced teachings of Lord Buddha, guru yoga is crucial to the development of our innate potential for perfection, enlightenment, and its essential meaning is expressed perfectly by the title of His Holiness's text: that the guru and the Buddha are to be seen as one. Pabongkha Rinpoche says in his *Liberation in the Palm of Your Hand*: "If the guru is not the Buddha, then who is?" And Lama Yeshe says in chapter 3, "By practicing guru yoga, you learn to understand that in reality, the guru is inseparable from the compassion and wisdom of Avalokiteshvara. Then you start to see the inseparability of these qualities and yourself."

Traditionally, before giving an empowerment into any tantric practice, the lama granting the empowerment, or initiation, gives teachings on the lamrim. The "Editor's Introduction" provides an overview of these teachings. In the "Prologue," Lama Yeshe introduces the concept of *mahamudra*, the essential teaching of the following commentary on the guru yoga of Avalokiteshvara, Chenrezig.

In "Part One: Lord Buddha's Teachings," Lama Yeshe describes the differences in approach between sutra and tantra. In "Part Two: Guru Yoga," Lama gives a verse-by-verse commentary on the text itself. In "Part Three: Mahamudra," he elaborates on the essential practice of guru yoga, leading practitioners through various meditations: how to become one with the guru-buddha, how to manifest oneself as Avalokiteshvara, how to recite the mantra, and so forth, all hinging upon mahamudra, the emptiness of one's mind. And in "Part Four: Mahamudra Is Always Here," Lama Yeshe explains how to trust our own wisdom and how to bring Lord Buddha's teachings into every minute of our lives.

Essentially, tantric meditation is sophisticated psychology: marvelous and radical methods for quickly perfecting the extraordinary potential for clarity, joy, compassion, and the other positive qualities that Buddha says are innate within all of us. It is easy to misunderstand tantra, however—and to mystify it. Lama Yeshe's genius is in his seemingly effortless ability to bring tantra down to earth without diminishing it, to make it real, to show us how to bring it into our everyday lives. If we treat our spiritual practice as some rarefied thing, Lama shows, then we are missing the point completely.

Lama Yeshe devoted most of his short life—he passed away in 1984 at the age of forty-nine—to guiding his students, the majority of whom are from the Western world. He met the first of them in the mid-1960s and, after establishing a monastery on Kopan hill near Kathmandu in Nepal, attracted thousands more to the courses he taught, there and around the world in the centers his students had established, until he passed away.

Lama Yeshe was unsurpassed in his qualities. Living his life as a humble monk, he was in reality "a great hidden yogi," according to Kyabje Zopa Rinpoche, his spiritual heir. And as a supreme communicator of Lord Buddha's views about the human experience, he made them utterly irresistible to his listeners. When Lama Yeshe taught, enlightenment was a real possibility.

MEDITATIONS

The ten meditations that Lama Yeshe guides the reader through are high-lighted throughout the text and listed altogether in appendix 2. There are eight steps, but each meditation does not necessarily cover all eight: one, for example, includes all except step 7, and another mentions only one step. Also, some meditations only briefly mention the steps, so, when doing these, flesh out the appropriate steps, taking them from meditation 1, which explains the visualizations most extensively, or from variations that Lama gives in the later meditations. In all cases, for step 2 one needs to refer to the practice, the *sadhana,* appendix 1. All meditations should be preceded by the prayers of refuge, bodhichitta, etc., in the sadhana. The words in bold type show the new visualizations that Lama adds to each meditation as the course progresses.

ACKNOWLEDGMENTS

These teachings were first edited in 1977, at Lama Yeshe's request, by Adèle Hulse. For the work on this present version, which started from scratch, the editor is grateful to the Lama Yeshe Wisdom Archive and Kopan Monastery for their support. A thousand thanks to Ven. Connie Miller and the Archive's Nick Ribush for each giving the manuscript a thorough going-over and clarifying many, many points; to Ven. Yeshe Chodron, Anjani O'Connell, and Tove Beatty for their proofing; to Jonathan Landaw for helping with the glossary; to Ven. Kathie Lobsang, Karen Meador, and Michelle Stewart for helping with the index; and to Tim McNeill, David Kittelstrom, Frank Allen, and Rod Meade-Sperry at Wisdom Publications for their enthusiasm.

Editor's Introduction

I prostrate to Atisha, keeper of the treasury of the teachings,
Whose faultless abridgement of its essential points summarizes
   and synthesizes for the first time since the prajñaparamita sutras
   of the Buddha
The two main paths of the Mahayana, the profound insight of emptiness
   and the vast action of bodhichitta,
In their correct order and proper lineages, from Buddha to Manjushri
   to Nagarjuna, on the one side, and from Buddha to Maitreya
   to Asanga, on the other.
                    From *Songs of Experience,* by Lama Tsongkhapa

IN ORDER TO BE QUALIFIED to receive an initiation into a tantric practice such as this yoga method, as Lama Yeshe would call it, and then to practice it, one needs to have a heartfelt appreciation for the three principal aspects of the path to enlightenment: renunciation, bodhichitta, and emptiness. An excellent way to accomplish this is to listen to and meditate upon the teachings known in Tibetan as *lamrim,* the "graduated path" to enlightenment.

In the lamrim—a packaging of Lord Buddha's teachings, unique to Tibet, based upon the elucidations of the eleventh-century Indian master Atisha— the essential points of Buddha's extensive explanations of psychology and philosophy are extracted and presented from A to Z in such a way that they can be internalized, experienced as something relevant to one's life. Which is the point. As Lama Tsongkhapa, the fourteenth-century founder of the Gelug tradition, according to whose approach Lama Yeshe's teachings are given, says in one of his poetic texts on the lamrim, *Songs of Experience,* "All the teachings are to be taken as sound advice as there is no contradiction between scripture and practice."

It is easy to be captivated intellectually by Buddha's ideas about reality but to forget to taste them, as Lama Yeshe would put it. It's also easy to not know *how* to taste them. The type of meditation that one uses to internalize these ideas, advocated by Lama Tsongkhapa, is called analytical meditation (Lama Yeshe touches on it briefly in chapter 10).

Simply, analytical meditation is a method for familiarizing oneself—the meaning of the Tibetan word for meditation, *gom*, is "to familiarize"—again and again with the various approaches taught by the Buddha, bringing them from the head to the heart, until they are one's own experience and no longer merely intellectual.

In other words, by sitting still and thinking about Buddha's views again and again and from many angles in a clear and intelligent way with a finely focused mind—in other words, by analyzing them—we are compelled to reassess at ever deeper levels the fundamental assumptions that we hold as truths and that Buddha has shown to be completely untrue. Eventually, we undergo a paradigm shift in the way we perceive ourselves and the world.

Buddha says that the extent to which these assumptions are out of sync with how things actually are is the extent to which we suffer and the extent to which, therefore, we harm others. Thus, a consequence of practice is the ending of suffering, *nirvana*—a psychological state, not some place like heaven.

The lamrim is presented according to three levels of practice. The first two scopes, as they are called, are practices shared by the Hinayana teachings of Lord Buddha, and the third scope is the presentation of the Mahayana components of the path to enlightenment.

According to Mahayana Buddhism, just as a bird needs two wings to fly, we need both the wing of wisdom and the wing of compassion. In order to develop the wisdom wing—mainly accomplished in the first two scopes—we work on our own minds; the main beneficiary is oneself, but indirectly others also benefit. In order to develop the compassion wing—accomplished in the third scope—we continue to work on our minds, but the main beneficiary is others.

THE PRELIMINARY CONTEMPLATIONS

Mind The first point to become familiar with—using the approach of Kyabje Zopa Rinpoche—is the beginninglessness of the mind. And especially for Westerners, this demands that we understand the nature of mind in a conventional sense. "The workshop is in the mind," as Rinpoche puts it, and as long as we're not clear about exactly what the mind is and what it is not, we won't make much progress in our practice.

According to Buddha, "mind" refers to the entire spectrum of our internal experiences: thoughts, feelings, emotions, tendencies, personality characteristics, unconscious, subconscious, intuition, spirit; all of this is known as mind, or consciousness. It is not the brain, it's not physical. It does not come from anyone else, neither one's parents nor a superior being.

The only other option is that it comes from previous moments of itself, that it has its own continuity, and thus is beginningless. This present moment of mind has to have come from a previous moment, which itself has come from a previous moment, and so forth. Like the chicken and the egg, we cannot find a first moment. No matter how far back we trace the continuity of our mental moments, whichever moment we get to, that moment can't simply have begun on its own, out of nowhere; it must necessarily have come from a previous moment of that very continuity of mind. Thus, we can never find a first moment. (And it's the same with physical energy, the universe itself. As His Holiness the Dalai Lama said in discussion with scientists: Big bang? No problem. Just not the first big bang, that's all.)

As a starting point for practice, it's also crucial to understand the ultimate nature of this mind of ours. According to Mahayana Buddhism, every living being possesses innately the potential for perfection, for buddhahood. The term in Tibetan for sentient being is *semchen*, literally, mind possessor; and according to Buddha there is not an atom of space where there are not sentient beings.

Each of these beings is actually a potential buddha (in Sanskrit, "fully awake") in the sense that an acorn is a potential oak tree. That is the acorn's nature, what it really is. We have no choice but to give it the appropriate conditions to enable it to become what it really is, an oak tree. And so with sentient beings: we have no choice but to develop our innate potential for perfection. That is to say, we can develop all our good qualities—such as love, compassion, generosity, wisdom, and so forth—to a state of perfection beyond which we can't develop them further. This state of perfection, Buddha says, is our natural state.

The Virtuous Friend Recognizing that we have this innate potential, we need to find someone to show us how to develop it. There's nothing we know that we haven't learned from others, so it goes without saying that to develop our perfection in the way that Buddha describes it, we need to find a qualified teacher.

Having found the teacher, we need to devote ourselves appropriately in order to get the maximum benefit from the relationship. In short, the heart of this practice is to see the guru as the Buddha.

It is said that the real benefit that comes from a teaching is not so much from the teacher's knowledge but more from our own confidence, our faith, that the teacher is the Buddha. And we will have this confidence only if we have thoroughly and intelligently checked the teacher before committing ourselves. If we're half-hearted, or overly sentimental, about this checking process, there will be no stability in the relationship, and we won't be convinced that the instructions are valid. We are moving into uncharted waters, so we need great confidence. The responsibility is ours.

This precious human rebirth Having found a teacher, we need to energize ourselves to want to develop our innate potential; the desire to do so doesn't come naturally. Lama Atisha, the eleventh-century Indian master who wrote the text *Lamp for the Path to Enlightenment* upon which Lama Tsongkhapa's lamrim teachings are based, recommends that we contemplate how fortunate we are that as human beings we have such excellent conditions: an intelligent mind, a healthy body, access to valid spiritual paths and teachers, and so forth; and that we are free of the appalling conditions that the vast majority of sentient beings experience.

This human life is a rare thing to have. According to Buddha, human beings represent only the tiniest percentage of all living beings. In *The Tibetan Art of Parenting*, one Tibetan lama was quoted as saying that whenever any human male and female are in sexual union, billions of consciousnesses that have recently passed away (from all realms of existence) are hovering around, desperate to get a human rebirth.

If we were to realize how hard we must have worked in our past lives to have obtained this good-quality, one-in-a-billion human body and mind and this collection of conducive conditions, we would be extremely humbled and would find it unbearable to waste even a single moment of this precious opportunity.

To waste this life is to use it for anything less than the practice of morality—and the minimum level of morality is to refrain from harming others. To use this life even more skillfully, we could remove from our minds the most deeply held wrong assumptions about how things exist; and, even more skillfully still, we could fulfill our innate potential for perfection by attaining buddhahood, and then be able to work unceasingly for the benefit of others.

THE FIRST SCOPE OF PRACTICE

Death and impermanence Having primed ourselves for practice, we now contemplate how this precious and rare human life is extremely fragile and can end at any moment. The assumption of permanence is deep within us. The idea that our friend who has cancer is dying and we are not is absurd. As Kyabje Zopa Rinpoche points out, "Living people die before dying people every day."

By contemplating that our death is definite, that our time of death is uncertain, and that the only thing of any use to us at death is the accumulation of virtue within our minds, we will radically increase our wish not to waste this life.

The suffering of the lower realms Given that we could die at any moment—"Best to think that I will die today," says Rinpoche—and given that there are countless imprints of negativity, the potential causes of future rebirths, on our beginningless minds, it is not unlikely that our next rebirth will be a suffering one. By contemplating the sufferings of such beings as animals, hungry ghosts, and hell beings, we can develop a healthy revulsion for those types of rebirth.

All living beings are experiencing the results of their own past actions. As Lama Yeshe says in chapter 2,

> It's not as if someone in a place called Hell built that iron house, lit the blazing fire, and thought, "Aha! I am waiting for Thubten Yeshe. Soon he will die and come here. I'm ready for him!" It is not like that. Hell does not exist in that way. The reality is that at the time of death, the powerful energy of the previous negative actions of that being, existing as imprints on its mind, is awakened, or activated, and creates that being's experience of intense suffering, which we call Hell. Hell does not exist from its own side; the negative mind makes it up.

Refuge in Buddha, Dharma, and Sangha Whom can I turn to to give me the methods to prevent such a suffering situation? We can have great appreciation for an excellent doctor, but if we're not suffering, we won't go out of our way to consult him. But when we discover that we're sick, we will eagerly turn to him and his medicine.

Recognizing that we're suffering, we contemplate the qualities of Buddha, his medicine, and his practitioners, and, based on our wish to get rid of suffering, we turn to them for support. Especially we turn to the Dharma, Buddha's medicine, the methods he taught that we will apply. The Dharma is the real refuge.

Karma Now we actually begin to practice: we apply Buddha's instructions on how to avoid suffering. We learn to know what to practice and what to avoid.

According to Buddha, everything we say, do, and think is a *karma*, an action, that will necessarily bring a reaction, a result, in the future. Every thought, word, and deed plants seeds in our minds that will necessarily ripen as fruit: negative actions ripen as suffering, positive actions ripen as happiness. There is nothing that living beings experience that isn't the result of what they've done before. With karma, there is no one sitting in judgment, punishing or rewarding us. Actions bring their own results; it just naturally happens, according to Buddha.

Given the simple logic that we want happiness and don't want suffering, we learn to abide by the laws of karma—natural laws, not created by anyone. What we are now is the result of what we have done, said, and thought before, and what we will be in the future is thus in our own hands. We are the boss. One might say that for the Buddha, karma is the creation principle.

It is not enough, however, merely to refrain from creating negative karma; we need to take care of the karmic seeds already in our minds, planted there since beginningless time. Thus, we begin to "have great respect and esteem for the four opponent powers, which can fully purify us of having to experience the results of our negative karma in the future," as Lama Tsongkhapa says in his *Songs of Experience*.

Given that we've had countless lives in the past and that many of the karmic seeds in our minds from those past lives are likely to be negative, and given that suffering comes from negative karma and that we don't want suffering, it follows that we would want to remove the negative karmic seeds from our minds before they ripen.

Purification is a psychological process. "We created negativity with our minds," says Lama Yeshe, "and we purify it by creating positivity." The four opponent powers are *regret*, *reliance*, the *antidote*, and the *promise*.

First, we need to *regret* the harm we've done in the past to others, because we do not want any more suffering in the future; we're fed up with suffering. Second, we need to *rely* upon the Buddha and his methods; we also rely upon the sentient beings whom we have harmed by developing compassion for them, aspiring to become a buddha as quickly as possible, since only then can we *really* know how to benefit them. Third, we apply the *antidote* in the form of a purification practice. This is like taking the medicine for our karmic ill-ness—and Buddhism has a medicine cabinet full of medicines. Finally, we make the *promise*, the determination not to create these negative actions, not to do harm, again.

"We can mold our minds into any shape we like," Kyabje Zopa Rinpoche says. We are "insane," he says, not to do this practice every day.

Having a strong appreciation for the logic of karma, based on thinking about death and impermanence and the lower realms and on going for refuge in the Buddha, his Dharma, and Sangha—all based on the preliminary three con-templations—we can be assured that, at the very least, when we die our con-sciousness will continue to experience an environment conducive to happiness.

Psychologically, this is the basic—but nevertheless amazing—level of prac-tice. A person of this level of capability is a mature human being possessing a healthy self-respect, who recognizes that their actions bring consequences to themselves, and who thus wants to avoid committing any negative actions. At this level of practice, there is not yet any talk of compassion for others— that belongs to the third scope. First, we need to develop compassion for ourselves.

This is the beginning of *renunciation*, the first principal aspect of the path to enlightenment.

THE SECOND SCOPE OF PRACTICE

At this point, we are now subdued enough, and aware enough, to delve more deeply into the way our mind works; to understand in a more sophisticated way Lord Buddha's model of the mind. We now truly become our own ther-apists, as Lama Yeshe would say. By familiarizing ourselves with the four noble truths, for example, we can fully develop renunciation.

The third noble truth is Buddha's assertion that it is possible to be free of suffering. This is another way of stating, according to the Mahayana Buddhist approach, that we all possess the innate potential for buddhahood.

So, if it's true that it's possible to be free of suffering—and Buddha is not talking the way most religions talk, that this can only be achieved after we've died, in heaven with God; he's talking psychologically—then we need to discover precisely what suffering is (the first noble truth), we need to discover precisely what the causes of suffering are (the second), and then we need to know the way to stop suffering and its causes (the fourth). It's extremely practical.

This needs a lot of inner investigation: the clarity, precision, and depth of analysis that we use in scientific discovery is what Buddha demands we use to discover the nature of our minds, karma, emptiness, and the rest.

There are three kinds of suffering: *the suffering of suffering*—ordinary, everyday suffering and pain; *the suffering of change*—what we usually think of as happiness; and *all-pervasive suffering*—the condition of being propelled into this universe, with this body and mind, all of which are products of desire and the other delusions, and thus are in the nature of suffering.

The causes of suffering are two: *karma,* our past actions that set us up to meet this suffering situation, and *the delusions,* our present neurotic responses to our situation. The punch in the nose, for example—which is what we normally think of as the cause of our suffering—actually plays only a secondary role, according to Buddha. My past harmful actions are the main reason I'm being punched now, and my angry response to the punch is the main reason I will suffer in the future. Thus, the ball keeps rolling. However, once we establish the actual causes of the problem, we will know how to solve it.

We need, then, to become very familiar with the way our mind works. We start by learning to distinguish between sensory consciousnesses and the mental consciousness. Then, within mental consciousness—our thoughts, feelings, and emotions—we need to distinguish between the positive states of mind and the negative. And then, crucially, we need to understand how all our emotions are conceptually based. Anger, attachment, jealousy, and the rest are elaborate conceptual constructions. They're stories made up by our minds.

The root cause of our suffering is the state of mind called *ignorance* (often known as *self-grasping* when it's related to oneself). Effectively, however, attachment is the main source of our problems in day-to-day life. It's the default mode of the mind. Yet, when we hear Buddha say that we can't be happy unless we give up attachment, we panic and think, as Kyabje Zopa Rinpoche puts it, "You mean, I have to give up my heart, my happiness?" This is because we confuse attachment with love, happiness, pleasure, and so forth.

The main cause of the second kind of suffering, *the suffering of change,* is attachment. The experience of pleasure I get when I eat chocolate cake is, in fact, nothing other than suffering. Why? First, the pleasure doesn't last: Attachment is completely convinced that it will, but the pleasure inexorably turns into suffering—the more cake I eat, the more disgusting it becomes. Second, the pleasure I experience is nothing other than suffering because it's adulterated, not pure. The pleasure is dependent upon delusions: I need to get something in order to be happy. And third, the pleasure is actually suffering because, as our mothers told us, "The more you get, the more you want." I don't actually get satisfaction when I eat the cake, which is what my attachment expects. In fact, I get dissatisfaction instead, as my yearning to eat cake is even greater next time.

Attachment goes to extremely subtle levels. It's insidious. As Lama Yeshe says, he could tell us about attachment "for one whole year," but we'll never begin to understand it until we've looked deeply and carefully into our own minds and discovered the intricacies of it for ourselves. Attachment is a honey-covered razor blade: we are convinced it's the prelude to pleasure, but in fact, it leads to nothing other than pain.

The pleasure we get by following attachment is the pleasure of the junkie: it doesn't last, it is contaminated, and it leads only to more craving. In our culture, it's the junkie who is said to have a problem with attachment while the rest of us are "normal." According to Buddha's model of the mind, attachment and addiction are synonymous. Due to our attachment, in other words, we're all addicts—it is simply a question of degree.

Buddha says that real pleasure, or happiness, is the state of our minds once we've given up attachment. It's our natural state (attachment, anger, jealousy, and the rest are thoroughly unnatural, according to Buddha), it lasts, and it isn't dependent upon something outside of ourselves. Who wouldn't want that?

Contemplating the four noble truths again and again will eventually bring us to a genuine renunciation of suffering and its causes. As Kyabje Zopa Rinpoche says, we will have achieved renunciation when "just the thought of another moment of attachment is so disgusting, it's like being in a septic tank."

The person at this level of capability is an extremely wise, joyful, loving person, and utterly content, regardless of whatever happens in their life.

This renunciation, the first of the three principal aspects of the path, is the culmination of practice of the first two scopes.

THE THIRD SCOPE OF PRACTICE

The accomplishment of renunciation is the sound basis for the development of love, compassion, and eventually, bodhichitta, the second principal aspect of the path. Without being fed up with my own suffering (renunciation), based on the understanding of why I'm suffering (my past karma and present delusions), I cannot develop empathy for the suffering of others (compassion) based on the understanding of why they're suffering (their past karma and present delusions).

The culmination of this scope of practice is the most sublime level of compassion, *bodhichitta:* the spontaneous and heartfelt wish to become a buddha as quickly as possible because the suffering of others is unbearable, knowing that only as a buddha can one be effective in eliminating the suffering of others.

Bodhichitta comes from the development of *great compassion:* not only is the suffering of others unbearable, but one feels the responsibility to remove it, just as a mother knows that it is her job to relieve the suffering of her child. His Holiness the Dalai Lama calls this great compassion *universal responsibility.*

Great compassion comes from *compassion,* the finding of the suffering of others unbearable.

Compassion is developed after *love,* which is the wish that others be happy. (Khensur Rinpoche Jampa Tegchog has pointed out that, depending on the person, sometimes compassion is developed before love.)

The foundation of all these is *equanimity,* the awareness that friend, enemy, and stranger are actually equal, from the point of view of their each wanting to be happy.

Of the various meditation techniques used to develop these amazing states of mind, the series known as exchanging self with others is considered to be the most powerful. Lama Atisha received these instructions of exchanging self with others from his guru Serlingpa in Indonesia. As Pabongkha Rinpoche points out in *Liberation in the Palm of Your Hand,* after Lama Atisha received these teachings, they were kept secret, as they were considered to be so far beyond the capability of most ordinary people.

Another way of developing bodhichitta, which comes from Lama Tsongkhapa, combines the techniques taught in exchanging self with others with those of the *sevenfold cause and effect instruction,* eleven altogether.

Equanimity Friend, enemy, and stranger are labels invented by the ego. A friend is necessarily a person who helps *me*—not my next door neighbor, me. An enemy is someone who harms me, and a stranger is a person who neither harms nor helps me. Consequently, we feel attachment for the friend, aversion for the enemy, and indifference toward the stranger. We are blinded by these views.

Until we can go beyond these deluded interpretations and come to see our enemies, friends, and strangers as equal, our hearts can't grow genuine love and compassion. As Kyabje Zopa Rinpoche says, the love we feel now (for our friends) is indeed love, but it's unstable because of being based on attachment. There are strings attached: as long as you help me, of course I will love you, that is to say, want you to be happy.

We need to argue with our ego's views, gradually seeing the illogic of them, discovering that in actual fact our friends, enemies, and strangers, from their point of view, are completely equal in wanting to be happy.

This equanimity is the stable foundation on which to build genuine love, compassion, great compassion, and bodhichitta.

We now meditate on the eleven techniques for developing bodhichitta.

All sentient beings have been my mother Recognizing that our mind is beginningless, it follows that we've had countless previous lives in which we have been connected to all beings countless times. It's a matter of numbers. This contemplation is a practical way to expand our mind to encompass all others.

In order to open my heart to these countless faceless beings, it helps to think about how they've all been my mother in the past. In the West, we might think this is meant to make us miserable, as we tend to think that our mothers are a main cause of our suffering. It's helpful, then, to contemplate the many ways in which our mother has been kind.

Contemplating the kindness of the mother At the moment, with our deeply held wrong assumptions—that I didn't ask to get born, that who I am has nothing to do with me, that my mother and father made me, and so forth—it seems reasonable to blame our parents for our problems.

Also, even our view of kindness is mistaken: we think of someone as kind only if they do what we want. However, if we understand that a person is kind when they make the effort to help us, then it's clear our mother has been kind in a myriad of ways. Even if she gave me away at birth, her kindness in not aborting me is extraordinary.

If all beings have been my mother, then they have all been kind to me in a vast number of ways.

Contemplating the kindness of all beings An even more profound way to expand our hearts to encompass others is to contemplate the ways in which *all beings* are kind to me. There's nothing that I've used in my life that hasn't come from the work of countless living beings. I can't find the beginning of the number of beings involved in the making of this book I'm holding: the trees the paper came from, the people who cut down the trees, the creatures who died, the people who shipped the trees, the driver of the truck, the people who made the truck; those who made the paper, who cut the paper, wrapped it, those who made the wrapping; those who built the store where I bought the book...If it were not for every one of them, I would not have a book, clothes, food, even a body.

Repaying their kindness I have no choice, then, but to try to repay the endless kindness of these countless mother sentient beings, but for whom I would have nothing. I would not even exist.

Seeing others and myself as equal Because of my delusions, instinctively I see my views, my needs, as more important than the views and needs of others. But there is no logic to this at all. In reality, there is not a fraction of difference between me and others, in just the same way as there is no difference between friend, enemy, and stranger. Everyone else wants to be happy and doesn't want to suffer, just like me. Just ask them; this fact is not hard to prove.

Even if I have low self-esteem, I don't really see others as more important than me; actually, I resent them. Always, I'm full of an overriding sense of self.

The disadvantages of cherishing myself more than others From the point of view of the wisdom wing, the main cause of our suffering is *self-grasping*, the instinctive clinging to an inherent sense of self. From the point of view of the compassion wing, the instinctive wish to take care of myself more than others—the attitude of *self-cherishing*—is the problem.

All my problems with others, in my personal relationships or at work, are because of putting myself first. Even in a relationship with another person in which I feel like the victim, this too is due to my past negative karma toward that person, which I created out of self-cherishing.

The advantages of cherishing others more than myself Everything good in my life comes from having put others first in the past: I have money because of my past generosity, people like me because I've been kind in the past, they trust me because I've spoken the truth. Putting others first is why I feel good right now.

If putting others first is what will make me happy, then how illogical of me not to do so. As His Holiness the Dalai Lama has said, "If you are going to be selfish, be wisely selfish: cherish others."

Taking upon myself the suffering of others: Developing compassion Using the meditation technique called *tonglen* (giving and taking), we visualize a suffering person or group of people in front of us. This technique can be done conjoined with the breath: when we breathe in, we imagine taking into ourselves the sufferings of others.

Pabongkha Rinpoche recommends that we start in the morning: after we rise, we visualize taking upon ourselves our own afternoon headache. Then we move on to taking on the sufferings of our dearest friends, then those of our enemies. Eventually, we take on the sufferings of all living beings in the various realms. We imagine that this suffering comes into us and smashes the rock of self-cherishing at our heart; as a result, we imagine that all others are now free of their suffering.

Giving my happiness and good qualities to others: Developing love When we breathe out, we imagine giving our happiness, wealth, health, good qualities, and merits to our friends, then to our enemies, and then to all living beings. How marvelous that they are now happy!

Great compassion On the basis of these meditations, we gradually become convinced that it's our job actually to take away the suffering of others. If not me, then who will do this? Contemplating in this way will eventually lead to the profound attitude of bodhichitta.

Bodhichitta Bodhichitta is the spontaneous and heartfelt wish to become a buddha as quickly as possible because only when we are enlightened will we be qualified to do the job of perfectly guiding others away from their suffering and to the perfection of their own buddhahood. One who has completely accomplished this sublime level of compassion, bodhichitta, is a *bodhisattva.*

One of the indications of having accomplished bodhichitta, of having become a bodhisattva, is that the thought of "I" no longer arises in the mind; thus, one exists only for the sake of others. It is said that even the breath of a bodhisattva is for the sake of others.

With this realization of bodhichitta, we will have accomplished the second of the three principal aspects of the path.

We now practice the six perfections of the bodhisattva: generosity, morality, patience, enthusiastic perseverance, meditation, and wisdom. The first four are accomplished in relation to sentient beings, the last two in one's meditation.

Generosity We practice this by giving things to those who need them, even as small as a mouthful of food to a dog; giving advice to help people's minds; giving what is called *fearlessness* by rescuing sentient beings from imminent death, for example, or by liberating people from prison, as Pabongkha Rinpoche suggests.

Sometimes it's easier to give advice than to give money to a homeless person, for example. We should learn to give what's difficult to give—and perhaps we could give five dollars, not fifty cents.

A sign of having perfected generosity is, for example, the ability to effortlessly give our body to a starving animal (assuming, of course, that there's no other supply of food available—bodhisattvas aren't trying to prove anything). In one of his previous lives, Lord Buddha happily gave his body to a starving mother tiger who was about to eat her babies. Right now, we're not even capable of giving, as Kyabje Zopa Rinpoche has said, "one tiny, tiny drop of blood to a mosquito."

Morality In our practice of the wisdom wing (the first and second scopes), we focus on the morality of refraining from harming others. In the practice of the third scope, the compassion wing, we focus on actively benefiting others as well: we work to help the homeless, the suffering, the sick, the poor, the dying—whoever crosses our path needing help.

Patience Patience is not merely gritting our teeth and waiting for unwanted things to go away. Patience is a courageous state of mind that happily welcomes the difficulty.

There are three types of patience. First, there's the *patience of accepting the harm that people do to us.* The main reason we get so upset is because of our deeply held wrong assumptions that it is unfair for others to harm me, that I don't deserve it, that it has nothing to do with me, and so forth—Lama Yeshe calls ego "the self-pity me." Buddha says it has everything to do with me: I created the cause to experience it, so I have no choice but to accept it. By thinking in this way, I purify my negative karma as well as develop a brave and happy mind.

There is also *the patience of accepting sickness, problems, and so forth that come to us,* for the same reasons as above. Kyabje Zopa Rinpoche says that "the thought of liking problems should arise naturally, like the thought of liking ice cream."

And finally, there is the *patience of gaining assurance in the Dharma,* as Pabongkha Rinpoche calls it.

Enthusiastic perseverance, or joyful effort Without enthusiasm, we can't succeed at anything in our lives, especially buddhahood. The main obstacles are the three kinds of laziness.

The first is the ordinary *laziness of being too tired.* We assume sleep is a necessity, but there are countless great practitioners who have gone beyond the need for it.

The second kind of laziness is what we usually call *being too busy:* putting off doing what we need to do. It feels like a virtue, but is, in fact, one of our biggest obstacles to success.

The third kind of laziness is the deeply held *belief that I'm not capable.* It, too, feels like a virtue; it seems as if we are being humble. But as long as we think that we can't achieve our potential, we will remain stuck in our comfort zone, never moving forward. In any case, it's simply not true: we all possess the potential to be a buddha. It's our nature.

Meditation *Calm abiding,* or *mental quiescence,* is the state of mind of a person who has achieved single-pointed concentration in meditation. There are two kinds of meditation, and this is the accomplishment of the first kind: concentration meditation.

Single-pointed concentration is a subtle level of conscious awareness, during which the grosser levels of conceptual and sensory awareness have necessarily ceased. It is a state of mind not even recognized in Western models of the mind, but one that Buddha says we can all access.

The main obstacles to our achieving calm abiding are the two extreme states of mind that we gravitate between during meditation: over-excitement and dullness. The person who has accomplished calm abiding has gone beyond even the subtlest levels of these two states. The mind when it's single-pointedly concentrated is extremely refined, very sharp and clear, and utterly still. Sensory awareness and gross conceptuality have completely ceased. The meditator can effortlessly access and stay in that state of mind as often and as long as they like. The experience of calm abiding is also an extremely joyful one—far more blissful, according to Lord Buddha, than the best sensory pleasure we've ever had.

Wisdom The essence of the perfection of wisdom is the development of *special insight* into emptiness. With the subtler level of conscious awareness gained in calm abiding meditation, we can identify and counteract the primordial misconception, the wrong assumption held deep in the bones of our being, about the way we ourselves and the world around us exist. This misconception is called *ignorance,* and keeps us locked into the cycle of suffering.

This ignorance is not merely unawareness of what's actually happening but a state of mind that actively makes up its own fantasies. It is impossible to see through the elaborate projections of ignorance with our usual gross conceptual level of mind; we need to access the microscope of our mind to do that, using the techniques of calm abiding.

As mentioned above, the extent to which we are not in touch with the way things are is the extent to which we suffer and, in turn, the extent to which we harm others. Ignorance, self-grasping, is the root neurosis, the primordial root cause of this suffering. Its main function is to cling to a separate, limited, and fearful sense of self, and its voices are attachment, jealousy, anger, pride, depression, and the rest. As long as we follow these, we are acting completely against our nature, Buddha says; we will always suffer, and we will cause suffering to others.

First, we need to comprehend the Buddha's explanations about the way ignorance and the other deluded emotions function and about the way the self and other things actually exist. Then, using the microscope of our mind, accessed in single-pointed meditation, we probe and analyze again and again in the second mode of meditation, called *insight meditation,* how this ignorance is a liar and a cheat: that it's been hallucinating the fantasy self all along.

In the subtlety of concentrated meditation we deconstruct ignorance's fantasies, eventually discovering, experientially and irreversibly, the absence of the fantasy self. As His Holiness the Dalai Lama has said, it's not as if we find the ego and then throw it out—it was never there in the first place. What we find is its absence. The discovery of this absence is the experience of emptiness.

With this, we will have accomplished the third principal aspect of the path, the view of emptiness.

So unbearable is the suffering of others, we will now happily embark upon the skillful practices of the Tantrayana, which will enable us to very quickly become our real self—a buddha.

BECOMING THE
COMPASSION BUDDHA

Avalokiteshvara, the buddha of compassion, in four-arm aspect.

Prologue
Mahamudra: Absolute Reality

THE ABSOLUTE SEAL

THERE ARE MANY DIFFERENT WAYS of analyzing and explaining Lord Buddha's marvelous teachings on the absolute reality of emptiness, *mahamudra*. Here, however, we will not be trying to understand the various philosophical points of view or to develop a merely intellectual understanding of mahamudra. We will try to achieve a direct experience of it.

Buddha explained mahamudra from two different perspectives: one according to the Paramitayana, his general Mahayana teachings (see chapter 1), the other according to the Vajrayana, his esoteric teachings (see chapter 2). *Maha* means great; *mudra* means seal; *mahamudra* means absolute seal, totality, unchangeability. Sealing something implies that you cannot destroy it. Mahamudra was not created or invented by anybody; therefore, it cannot be destroyed. It is absolute reality.

I see Western scholars talking in extensive philosophical terms about mahamudra and the rest, but I have a question for them: "You talk about these things, but do you meditate?" Sometimes, our mind is interested only in fantasy, which is like going to the supermarket with empty pockets, saying, "This is fantastic. That is good. This is healthy. That is tasty." In the end, you have nothing.

The intellectual world and the practical, experiential learning process are as different as a supermarket and Mount Everest. If you leave mahamudra at the intellectual level, it will never touch you; it will have nothing to do with you. Even if you write an entire book about mahamudra, nothing can stop your problems; nothing can move your wrong conceptions.

But don't worry, I'm not going to talk about mahamudra too intellectually. I'm going to keep it simple.

MAHAMUDRA EMBRACES ALL PHENOMENA

Lord Buddha explained that mahamudra refers to the unborn, unchangeable nature that exists within all phenomena. It is not as if mahamudra is something special that exists only in some holy place and not in your breakfast muesli. Mahamudra exists within all phenomena without discrimination. Its nature is reality-nature. That's why Lord Buddha says, *chönam kungyi rangzhin chaggya chen:* the absolute nature of all phenomena is the great seal. This mahamudra character embraces all phenomena in samsara and nirvana.

Absolute nature is not some philosophy made up by Lord Buddha or by Nagarjuna, the great Indian master who clarified emptiness. Nobody can invent the absolute nature of reality. But even though mahamudra is the nature of all universal phenomena, our hallucinating, conceptual mind prevents us from seeing it. Instead of seeing totality, we get caught up in relative notions of reality. We have a fanatical, dualistic view of how things are.

That is why the conception, the concrete projection, of the self, "I," appears to our mind; and it appears as totally independent, as a self-entity. Therefore, even if we know about mahamudra, we don't really know at all; we don't realize the interdependent nature of phenomena.

Check up on the ego's view of the I when you're feeling hungry. In reality, your hunger depends on many interdependent phenomena: there is the kitchen…the food…your body and mind…all these things are dependent on each other. If you realize that your hungry I is totally dependent, you'll be able to control your hunger, and after eating, you will have a deeper understanding as well.

When one part of an interdependent combination disappears, the combination itself disappears as well. For example, in our group of seventy people here, when one person disappears, the group of seventy has also gone; the group of seventy no longer exists. Do you agree or not? It's so simple, so logical. If you remove one of a hundred butter lamps, the group of a hundred has gone as well, because the group of a hundred is the combination of each one.

Looking at it another way, even as you are eating your muesli, as your stomach gets full, you're thinking, "Oh, the hungry I feels better now." But even that is a misconception. You are still holding onto the previous hungry I, even though it has disappeared. Maybe this is difficult for you to understand. It's not surprising that many Buddhist professors misinterpret Nagarjuna's view and think that he is nihilistic, that he destroys everything.

Check up. The "you" of this morning has disappeared, but you still think it exists this evening. Similarly, you think that the baby "you" still exists today. But even after one second, the "you" of that previous second has already disappeared. Everything—yourself, your sense perceptions, all the objects of your senses, everything—is in the nature of change; we can say, in fact, that everything disappears.

The idealistic ego thinks, "I built this meditation hall," for example. But the you who built the *gompa* (meditation hall) has already disappeared. The gompa, the making of the gompa, and the person who made it—this relationship—have all disappeared.

Here's another example. When it is getting dark, you see a hose rolled up and think it is a snake. Suddenly, you're afraid, "Oh!" That's a good example. Because of the conditions—darkness and the rolled-up hose—you get the idea that there's a snake there. The combination of factors brings about the wrong conception, and you feel afraid, perhaps even more afraid than if you'd seen a real snake in the distance. This time, because it is so close, you have this hallucination.

This is a good example of how we hallucinate. This snake does not even exist, but your mind paints a picture, creates a fantasy, makes it up. Nevertheless, there is an interdependent relationship of environment, object, and many other things.

It's the same with the hungry I, the concrete I: it's also an ego-projection, just as the snake is. Although the I does not exist within your five aggregates—your body and mind—it looks like it does; it appears to be concretely existent. The I seems to exist somewhere within your sense organs, but it appears to your sense perception and your conceptual mind in exactly the same way as the hallucination, or projection, of the snake appears.

Using penetrative wisdom to look mindfully into the situation, you will never find anything that you can point to and say, "This is the snake." You will never find it. You can't. It's the same with the I, the hallucinated concrete idea of a self-existent I. When penetrative wisdom checks up, it cannot find the I anywhere within your body—not in your heart, your brain, your leg, your hand, or anywhere else.

Outside this gompa, there are some logs of wood. If we look with penetrative wisdom, we cannot find "Tom" within the energy of that wood. It's exactly the same if we look within the energy of Tom's five aggregates: his body and mind. No matter how much we search, from head to foot or from foot to head, we can never say, "*This* is Tom; here he is." You can never find any "Tom."

You always think you are something; you are not satisfied with just your name. You seek some reality, some identity, beyond the name. However, the fact is that besides the name "Tom," nothing else exists.

There is not much difference between the logs of wood and Tom's aggregates. Of course, the aggregates have some kind of interdependent relationship with Tom that they do not have with the wood outside, but in the end, "Tom" and "wood" are merely names.

Here's another example: Before the name "Peter," for example, is given to a child, one would not say, "There's Peter" when looking at that child's body. Yet, once you have named your baby "Peter," automatically, when you look at his body, you think, "Peter." You don't remember that *you* gave the name "Peter." Instead, you think that "Peter" comes from the side of the person, from out there. Such concrete attachment to such a concrete object!

It's the same when some situation bothers you. You think, "This is bad." Actually, you have made that situation bad; you have created it by labeling it "bad." No such concretely "bad" situation exists. You have named the situation "bad" in the same way that you have named the baby "Peter."

All our judgments are very gross. We see things as having a very gross nature; we never see them in their nature of totality. Therefore, we need to meditate in order to investigate the totality nature of all phenomena.

THERE IS ONLY NAME

Other religions, Hinduism and Christianity, for example, assert a soul, some kind of permanent entity, which possesses all the goodness of the human being. But Buddhism would say that from a philosophical point of view it is actually impossible that such a solid, concrete entity exists. There is no such concrete soul, spirit, or whatever you want to call it; there is no such permanent, independent entity existing within the human being, not even relatively.

At some point in history on this earth, people thought that there had to be some concrete, solid entity, something self-existent, in order for there to be such a thing as a human being. Such a philosophy was created in order to be able to say, "This is a human being." So when Nagarjuna came along and vanquished such conceptions, people thought that he was nihilistic: "Oh, don't go near him; he'll turn you into a nihilist!" Even many Buddhist traditions still have difficulty accepting Nagarjuna's view.

But you can see: there are many interdependent parts, you give a name to that combination, and then those parts become that object. Nagarjuna would say that it's the same with every existent thing: there is just the name. There is no happiness, no unhappiness. He says that if you really check, if you penetratively investigate the situation, the object, it is impossible to find anything.

Take the pain in your body, for example. When you search for the pain with penetrative wisdom in the area where the energy of the pain is, sometimes the pain disappears. I'm sure that you have had this experience. Even if you just make up the idea, "Oh, my knee is blissful," sometimes you will feel bliss. You check up. Good and bad come from the idea, the concept. No such thing actually exists.

All these examples show how ridiculous we are. Everything is just a name. The more superstition there is, the more names we produce. And because there is more superstition in the West, there are more names, more things, more goodness in the supermarket!

A mirage is a good example. I have had the experience sometimes that when I am thirsty and I see a mirage, there appears in my mind a very concrete image of cold, calm water. We all know that a mirage is a totally interdependent phenomenon: a combination of the vibrations of the sun and the sand creates this type of energy, a mirage. But when you look at it, because it appears as if water were really there, suddenly clean, clear water appears to your mind.

This is a good example of how things don't have solid existence. A mirage appears to have a very solid existence, doesn't it? But if you check up, it is merely the coming together of various conditions: an interdependent phenomenon, changing, changing all the time. It is actually the same with everything in the world.

PHENOMENA DO EXIST—INTERDEPENDENTLY

Nevertheless, the various phenomena do exist. When we describe how things are mere names, this does not mean that we are being nihilistic and are destroying phenomena; we are not saying that phenomena do not exist. When you contemplate the right view, the hallucination, the fantasy of the self-existent object that your conceptual mind believes in, automatically disappears. When this happens, your wisdom experiences what we call right view: emptiness, voidness, or in Sanskrit, *shunyata.*

At the beginning of your contemplation of right view, use your intellect to examine the ways in which phenomena are interdependent, how they come together in dependence upon various things. Then, when you gain an experience of this, do not intellectualize. Just leave it there; let go. When this wisdom is there, it is a very powerful experience.

Normally, we see the world as concrete. When you go to Sydney, for example, and see the fantastic buildings, it all seems so concrete, so solid. But when you experience emptiness, right view, the whole world becomes like nothingness, so small. Of course, it is not small, but because you are controlling the heavy vibrations that produce all the fantasies, it appears like nothingness.

Nagarjuna explained this reality in his philosophical writings, strongly emphasizing how phenomena do exist, that we are not destroying reality, nor are we saying that there is nothing. Everything does exist as an interdependent phenomenon, even if only in name. If you understand this properly, you will understand that Nagarjuna's view is not at all nihilistic.

The Tibetan term for interdependence is *tendrel.* Each time a thing appears to us or a situation arises, we say, "This is this, this is that." But the moment we have said it, it has already changed.

SO MUCH FEAR

Thus, we can see that delusions arise when our sense perceptions make contact with an object. Interdependent phenomena come together, and suddenly delusion arises, such as when we mistake the rope for a snake and feel very afraid and emotional. In fact, this is a fantasy, a projection of our mind. In the same way, all universal phenomena are actually projections of the mind, fantasies projected by the mind.

However, the conceptualizing ego always feels that there is something more than what is made up by the mind. But when you check up, intensively investigate the object—the snake, for example—the hallucination disappears. When you realize that it is only your mental projection, your fear is automatically released.

It's interesting that the phenomena that look so real to us are merely interdependent combinations of things; they're all made up. When one of the factors disappears, the whole thing disappears. But until we discover mahamudra—all-embracing unity, reality—everything we experience with our sense perceptions, or even in our dreams, will be a hallucination. We always feel that objects are self-entities that don't depend on mental projection, but everything in the sense world is a hallucinated bubble—it comes from nothingness, formlessness, and its nature is such that it will disappear into nothingness, emptiness, formlessness. Nevertheless, we sentient beings believe in a concrete world filled with concrete self-entities.

We feel insecure; we have so much fear. This comes from our lack of understanding, our "ignorance," which means not understanding right view, reality. People often say, "I don't believe in anything," thinking that only religious people are "believers." This is common in the West. In fact, when you have the hallucinated vision of the snake and feel afraid, it shows with perfect logic that you *do* believe in something. Intellectually, you might say, "I don't believe in anything," but in fact, you believed the hose was a snake. If you didn't, why were you afraid? If you're a true nonbeliever, why did fear arise when you saw the fantasy of the snake?

This shows that you have tremendous belief. As long as you hallucinate, there is always belief. Belief is not just an intellectual thing. Simultaneously, each misconception in our mind is accompanied by various states of mind: feeling, discrimination, cognition, and so forth. These mental factors are automatically there, watching. Therefore, as long you have wrong conceptions, hallucinations, there is always feeling.

People ask, "What's the best solution for fear?" Here are two methods that are among the most powerful ways to overcome fear. The first is to cultivate more concern for other sentient beings' pleasure than for your own. This attitude lessens fear. The second solution is right view, wisdom, which completely cuts all fear. Fear comes from the unclear fantasy mind, which produces speculation and superstition. Actually, this is the nature of fear.

It's the same when you worry, when you are thinking about something that you don't have. This, too, comes from not having right view. Instead of worrying, try to understand and simultaneously just to act; then you will get what you want. Right now, we don't put our actions in the right direction; we worry instead. We speculate so much, it's as if we're in a dream state.

The right view of wisdom is blissful. This is easy to understand: the nature of wisdom is bliss because it automatically releases agitation, fear, and worry. If you are free of those emotions, you feel naturally joyful, don't you? In actual fact, emptiness is always there—you just need to recognize it.

You always feel you want a happy life. Well, the happy life is always there—you just need to recognize it. Sentient beings are too much. They're always wanting something, but looking nowhere. Eventually, when you really see this, you'll laugh instead of worry. Up in the mountains, Tibet's great yogi Milarepa was laughing at the world. He couldn't control it because he saw reality. When you see reality, you, too, will always be laughing. Whenever you see everything in a concrete way, it's too heavy; you can't laugh. With wisdom, you can control the whole world.

When you perceive the reflection of yourself in a mirror, you feel light. In the same moment that you see your image, you instinctively know that it is not the real you. This is a good example. All existent phenomena, the objects of the sense world, are like a reflection in a mirror. When you understand right view, reality, all relative phenomena somehow become lighter for you. Maybe you see it, but maybe you don't see it. Let's say there is some desirable chocolate, and someone says, "Do you see the chocolate?" The person who understands right view, the reality of this chocolate, could say both yes and no. Why would you say yes? Because relatively, the chocolate is there. Why would you say no? Because it has no concrete self-entity.

When there is that heavy feeling, chocolate seems huge, but when you see reality, it's as if you're seeing through the energy of the chocolate, as if you're seeing it through a veil. It's not too heavy; there is no concrete vision of it.

If you look at an iron door with right view, instead of seeing heavy iron, you see it as very light and feel as if you could walk straight through it. You can have that kind of experience, and it's scientific. In reality, when you check up, an iron door is simply a combination of atoms, electrons, and other particles. Even without the experience of emptiness, without mahamudra, if you check up on the nature of such phenomena scientifically, your concrete conceptions will become lighter.

When you understand the Paramitayana explanation of right view, you can easily understand the tantric view of mahamudra. "But mahamudra is universal; reality is the same," you might say. That's true, but the Paramitayana view is much easier to experience than that of the Vajrayana.

Here, for example, when we practice the tantric mahamudra of Vajrayana, we visualize ourselves in the clear-light nature of the divine deity Avalokiteshvara's body. Our energy becomes Avalokiteshvara, and simultaneously we experience bliss and understand emptiness. This combination is difficult. Why? Generally, when we are blissful, we lose our mindfulness, our penetrative wisdom; we become as if unconscious. Check for yourself. When you are happy, you are intoxicated by sentimental feelings; even if somebody wants to talk to you, you don't even notice them. You are completely full of yourself. Through practicing yoga methods such as this, you learn to have a clean-clear vision of yourself as the deity and simultaneously to experience bliss and intensive, mindful right view. This is the mahamudra of tantric yoga.

PART ONE
Lord Buddha's Teachings

1 ~ Sutra: Rejecting Delusion

HINAYANA AND MAHAYANA

LORD BUDDHA gave many different teachings, in accordance with the different levels and needs of sentient beings' minds. It is said that he gave 84,000 teachings as the solutions to the 84,000 delusions. If somebody wanted to gain a mere intellectual understanding of all these methods within their lifetime, it would be almost impossible; however, since enlightenment within a single life is possible, one can not only understand all these teachings intellectually but totally realize them as well.

Take, for example, the gradual path to liberation, the lamrim. It has three different divisions that accord with the three different levels of motivation that sentient beings have for practicing Dharma. Some people want simply to ensure that they get another human rebirth in their next life; others seek only the small liberation of nirvana. Emphasizing that people with these two levels of motivation should focus on releasing their own attachment and delusions, Lord Buddha gave them Hinayana teachings.

Then there are those who are more advanced. Even though they understand their own delusions, they are not particularly concerned with eradicating them or gaining quick liberation for themselves alone. They are far more concerned about the happiness of others, of all universal living beings. Lord Buddha gave such people Paramitayana teachings—the great compassion of bodhichitta—and the other general Mahayana teachings of the bodhisattva's path. Within the Mahayana there are others who are even more advanced, the most intelligent and fortunate ones. Lord Buddha gave them the esoteric Vajrayana teachings. We call such people precious jewels, or precious disciples.

You might think, "I must be at only one of those three levels. Why doesn't Lama just teach me that one?" but that's not how it works. The explanations of one level alone are not enough to lead you all the way to enlightenment. You need gradually to receive all three. Then, acting gradually and continuously, you actualize the first level, then the second, and finally the third.

Whether we call them the 84,000 teachings or the three divisions, everything Lord Buddha taught can be divided into Hinayana and Mahayana. *Yana* is Sanskrit and means vehicle. If, for example, you want to cross a body of water, you get in a boat, and it carries you to the other side. The Mahayana attitude of bodhichitta is like a boat. If you get into that vehicle, it will automatically carry you to enlightenment.

Those most suited to Hinayana, the Small Vehicle, on the other hand, gain an understanding of their own problems and develop an enthusiastic wish to reach self-realization for their own purpose. That attitude carries them to their goal, self-liberation, or nirvana.

The Mahayana, the Great Vehicle, has two divisions. The first is the causal vehicle; the second, the effect, or resultant, vehicle. The causal vehicle is the Paramitayana, or Perfection Vehicle, which is sometimes called the *Sutrayana*, or Sutra Vehicle. It explains the path to enlightenment through the gradual development of bodhichitta and the six perfections of the bodhisattva.

The result vehicle is the Vajrayana—Tantrayana, or tantra. We call it *result vehicle* because the yogi or yogini who actualizes tantric methods brings the result, enlightened action, into the present. The experience of the Buddha's enlightened action is brought directly into the gradual path to enlightenment, right now.

When you receive an initiation into the practice of Chenrezig, Avalokiteshvara, you transform your energy, your consciousness, into Avalokiteshvara, here and now; you become Avalokiteshvara (see page 43). Instead of thinking, "Impossible! I'm absolutely impure, deluded; I can't be Avalokiteshvara," you transform your ordinary body, speech, and mind into the blissful wisdom of the divine, Avalokiteshvara, total enlightenment experience. You bring that enlightened experience into the path to liberation right now.

You can see within yourself how the lamrim works. The explanations at the beginning of the lamrim place much emphasis on your own everyday actions. When you begin to see all your inner garbage, you start to feel that you are entirely in the nature of negativity. You feel hopeless. But as you continue to practice the lamrim, you gradually begin to think about all living beings instead of only about your own ego-puzzles, conflicts, and delusions. You become more open. Your mind becomes more universal, less narrow. As your attitude changes, so does the vehicle within you.

Sometimes people talk about three categories of vehicle—Hinayana, Paramitayana, and Vajrayana. This can lead you to think that Vajrayana is different from Mahayana, but that's not right. Both Paramitayana and Vajrayana are Mahayana vehicles; each can carry you to enlightenment. They do not bring different results; there are different vehicles because Lord Buddha taught different methods for different levels of practitioner. Both Paramitayana and Vajrayana lead you to enlightenment, but one is slower, the other quicker. Tantra is the vehicle that carries you most quickly to enlightenment.

Both Hinayana and Paramitayana assert that we are caught in samsara—suffering in cyclic existence—because of delusion and karma. Therefore, these must be rejected. Tantra, however, maintains that we continuously circle through samsara because our perception of reality is ordinary rather than divine. When we develop a more refined view and continuously hold in our consciousness a vision of beauty and perfection, there's no way that depression or selfishness can arise. However, we have to develop this experience through practice; we can't just leave it at the intellectual level.

THE ADVANTAGES OF CLEAR UNDERSTANDING

If you have a clear understanding of the entirety of Lord Buddha's teachings and methods, you will be comfortable with what you are doing, and nobody will be able to disturb your practice. If you don't, even though you may have a degree of right understanding, clever intellectuals will be able to shake your confidence, and your faith might disappear. Even though what you are doing is right, you might start to feel, "I must be doing something wrong. He challenged my practice and I couldn't respond."

It is not always easy in this world. Some professor can come up to you and say, "So, you study meditation?" and then, using words that you don't understand, start talking to you about various philosophies. You know what he means but can't quite put it together. Then, you start thinking that you don't know anything, and you give up even the little meditation you do: "I'm hopeless. I can't do anything. That professor completely caught me out."

We all sometimes feel like this. Therefore, you should try to understand the entire lamrim, both Sutrayana and Tantrayana, from beginning to end. Then you'll be able to actualize your meditations easily, without obstacles.

Lord Buddha taught many different things in dependence upon the different levels of mind of his disciples. He said, "Sometimes I say 'yes,' sometimes 'no,' so don't take my words literally. Use your wisdom to analyze what I say." It is your own wisdom that becomes your liberation.

2 ~ *Tantra: Using Delusion*

THE QUALIFICATIONS FOR PRACTICING TANTRA

IN THE TIBETAN TRADITION, we emphasize the development of renunciation, bodhichitta, and the wisdom of emptiness as the foundation of the practice of tantra. We call these three *preliminary practices* because they are prerequisites for receiving teachings on tantra. If you don't understand these three principal aspects of the path or the nature of delusion, then, when you hear teachings on, for example, the tantric technique of taking the energy of desire into the blissful path of liberation, you can easily find yourself in trouble.

The practice of tantra is powerful. Tantra is the quickest path to enlightenment. But if you are not qualified, it is also the most dangerous. We liken tantric practice to a snake inside a hollow bamboo tube. It can only go up or down; there's nowhere else to go. It can't go sideways. Tantra is a bit like that.

MISTAKEN IDEAS ABOUT BUDDHIST TANTRA

There are many misleading books on Tibetan Buddhism and Buddhist tantra in the West. According to some writers' completely mistaken ideas, tantra has to do only with sex. They think they can understand something just by looking at it. Other people think that Tibetan Buddhism is some kind of magic, and some fear that Tibetan lamas will control their minds. I've been really surprised by the assumptions some people make.

There are certain higher levels of Buddhist tantra in which the energy of male and female in union is used, but this is highly advanced and very rare. In worldly terms we would consider such a situation one of craving, but skillful beings can transform that energy into the blissful path to liberation. That can definitely be done.

Another misunderstanding confuses Buddhist with Hindu tantra. While both traditions use the word "tantra," the meaning in each case is different.

There may be superficial similarities between certain practices, but you cannot say they are the same.

Some of the early European travelers to the East did not make contact with the right people. When they saw Tibetan tantric art in temples, they thought that what they saw was Tibetan Buddhism and that they could understand it just from that. Then they wrote their misconceptions in books, thus spreading them to others.

These days, however, people do more than just look. They check closely and try to gain experience. Also, good translations of Tibetan Buddhist teachings are now becoming more available. Things are coming together to give people a much better understanding. This is important.

MAKING ORDINARY ACTIONS DIVINE

The powerful path of tantra takes all the energy of desire and, instead of rejecting it like poison, brings it into the path of liberation. Normally, we avoid poison as much as we possibly can, but in tantra we use it as a powerful medicine.

Tibetan doctors use many different natural substances, including poisons, to make medicine. In this way, poison can become highly beneficial. I'm sure that Western medicine once did the same thing, but today, chemicals have probably made the use of poison in medicine unnecessary.

If all you've studied up to now has been lamrim, you can see that tantra has an entirely different approach to Dharma practice. The lamrim teaches you to renounce and reject attachment, anger, jealousy, and so forth. Perhaps you're now starting to think, "These lamas are crazy. Sometimes they squeeze me by saying, 'If you follow desire, you will create negative karma and experience only suffering.' Now they're saying, 'It's okay to follow desire. Take it into the path and it will liberate you.'" Now you probably don't know *which* path to take.

However, taking the energy of desire into the path does not mean that you can just do whatever you like. It means that instead of trying to escape any situation that arises, you can now deal skillfully with it. You can transform everything that arises in your everyday life—every condition and situation, all your desire—into the path to liberation. Instead of bringing you down, any kind of negative energy can now help you reach enlightenment. But you should check this through your own experience, not just through my words.

Still, you can now see why we say that tantra can be dangerous. Even transforming the simple pleasure of your breakfast muesli: you can do it, but you have to practice constantly—from morning to night and from sleep to awakening—transforming everything you do into pure action.

Think about how you are when you get up most mornings. "I'm cold; I'm hungry; I'm suffering," and your mind goes straight into your coffee. Instead of starting your day like that, imagine that Avalokiteshvara is there beside you, waking you up by sending powerful, radiant white light directly into your consciousness. Then he sinks into you, and suddenly you become Avalokiteshvara. Motivate: "I am very lucky still to be alive this morning, so today I will transform all the energy of my body, speech, and mind into the blissful path of liberation. May everything I do become a divine action of Avalokiteshvara." Dedicate everything you do to the benefit of all sentient beings. It takes only a few moments to start the day by thinking this way.

Then, get up with a mantra, and transform everything else you do. When you wash, imagine that you are washing your divine body with blissful energy instead of washing your mundane, suffering body with water. Then, dress your divine body with blissful, divine robes instead of with ordinary clothes. If you start your morning like that, the rest of your day will be much easier.

After that, when you go to breakfast, bless everything that you eat and drink so that it becomes blissful, radiant light energy. Then, offer it to divine, universal, compassion-wisdom Avalokiteshvara. But *you* are Avalokiteshvara; Avalokiteshvara is not outside of you. Or, if you prefer, you can visualize Avalokiteshvara in your heart, or you can make your offering to Guru Avalokiteshvara—the guru seen as inseparably one with Avalokiteshvara. From the moment you wake up, you should transform everything.

This whole process has to do with awakening our mind. Our usual actions are like those of a cow, but when we transform them, they become divine and beyond normal conceptions. Of course, if we do not have some understanding of the nature of reality, emptiness—that things don't exist as self-entities—it is difficult to transform ordinary energy into blissful energy. But for those who understand emptiness, it is easy.

When you transcend ordinary experience, each time you drink, for example, you energize your Avalokiteshvara nervous system, and this blissful experience brings you psychological satisfaction. When you bless your food at lunchtime and transform it into the universal blissful energy of the divine view of Avalokiteshvara's divine consciousness, you completely change the relationship between the physical energy of the food and yourself. Try it, and you'll experience what I'm telling you.

Normally, you consider eating and drinking to be mundane: "I don't like my body. I don't want to eat this stuff but I have to. Ugh!" Sometimes you don't like your own actions. That's not right. But when you transform them into Avalokiteshvara's blissful wisdom energy, it's entirely different; everything changes. You're a different person; your mind becomes something else.

Often, when we eat, we stand around busily talking. If possible, however, you should sit down and take your time. Here, at this retreat, it doesn't matter if you're part of a group. Just go off by yourself, sit down, and relax, instead of socializing as if you were at a party. If you learn to do this correctly, then later, when you're at a party, you can make your actions transcendent and transform them into the blissful path of liberation.

At the beginning of your training, spontaneous action is not instinctive. It's difficult; it requires effort. When you have developed beyond effort, however, you don't need gross levels of thought to do something; your actions become spontaneous.

It's the same when you are in bed, trying to go to sleep: your mind is all over the place. "After this meditation course I'm going there to do this, and he says I must do that, and she is this and this…" It's too much! You're flying around the world, going all over Sydney and Melbourne, going to parties. Psychologically, you are so busy. So naturally, when you get up in the morning, you are very tired. This is what mental energy is like—you're not doing anything physically, but mentally you're on some fantastic trip.

So, when you sleep, become Avalokiteshvara. If you have difficulty sleeping, concentrate on the syllable *Hrih* at your throat chakra, or at your heart if you like. Visualize it vibrating, and radiating black light. Black? Yes; or at least, very dark. In the West, when you want to sleep you close the curtains to make it dark, don't you? You can't sleep if it's light because your mind is busy; it wants to look at things. During sleep, the sense organs' perceptions are not functioning. So this is a method to use if you want to sleep—all day and all night if you like! There are many technical methods like this in tantra.

For example, some men have difficulty controlling their sexual energy when they're asleep, especially during a meditation course like this, and lose sperm. If, with strong concentration, you can bring the seed syllable *Hrih* to your throat, there's no way you can lose that energy. When we go to sleep, the energy of our subtle nervous system moves downward. You see, it's not only psychological; physiologically, things happen that create a situation for the mind. But techniques such as this can trick your mind. When you place your concentration at your throat and bring the energy up, it stays there, and you do not lose it.

Instead of looking at others and thinking, "She is this, he is that," visualize them as Avalokiteshvara. When you visualize other people as Avalokiteshvara, there's no way you can feel negative toward them. It's impossible. Instead of misery, they give you blissful energy. Then everything—situations, your environment, your mandala—becomes pure energy: totally pure, blissful wisdom.

When you meditate in this temple, instead of thinking of it as made of ordinary wood, imagine that blissful, universal compassion in the form of radiant light emanates from you as Avalokiteshvara, or from Guru Avalokiteshvara. Then when you look at the walls, they give you a joyful vibration rather than an I-don't-like-this-wood vibration.

You have already had some experience of this. Check up how you are in your own home or with your friends. By referring to your own everyday experiences, you can understand how it can be possible to expand and develop them infinitely.

WHAT IS REALITY?

I am not talking about things that are impossible to develop. Tantra fits the Western mind, which is a tricky, technical mind. Since tantra has technical methods, I think the Western mind can digest it easily. You like beauty, good smells, lovely forms and colors, don't you? You like to decorate, to have nice things, to transform things, to decorate your houses this way and that. It is the same with tantra, but we use the mind instead, that's all.

Perhaps you think I'm saying that you have to hallucinate, to make something up that has nothing to do with reality; or that tantra makes you become a magician so that you invent something. "This is not reality," you think. "How does this work?"

Let me ask you a question. What is reality? Is your vision of desirable chocolate reality? When you have problems and conflicts and see people as miserable, is that reality or not? I tell you, everything that you consider good or bad, the entire sensory world, is your own psychological invention. Your mind makes it up. Nothing that exists in this world is absolutely, automatically good or bad. That is impossible.

Chandrakirti, the famous Indian Mahayana saint who expounded Nagarjuna's Madhyamaka philosophy, gives the following example. Imagine there is one cup of liquid, and three different beings are looking at it. One is a human being, one is a samsaric god, and one is a *preta*, a hungry ghost. Although they are all looking at the same object, the same cup of liquid, each one sees it entirely differently. The human being sees it as water; the god sees it as blissful nectar, *amrita;* the hungry ghost sees it as blood or pus. So, what is reality? Whose perception is correct?

Another example: Each man chooses the woman he likes according to his own particular point of view. And according to their own view of good and bad, women make their choices of men. If you think about it, how can you make someone beautiful or ugly? It's all made up by the mind. You check up. You like or dislike someone not because they are good or bad by nature but because you have a fixed idea, a preconception, of how they should be. You respond automatically: "good" or "bad."

This is another way of saying that you are not liberated. Your conflicts with others are the result of your fanatical, fixed ideas of good and bad. You don't have universal understanding; your fanatical view prevents the growth of your universal wisdom and compassion, the essence of Avalokiteshvara.

Lama Je Tsongkhapa's answer to Chandrakirti's debate is that existing simultaneously in that cup of liquid is the reality of water, the reality of blissful nectar, and the reality of blood. How? Because the imprints of powerful karmic energy that are latent within each being are awakened by the cooperative cause, the sight of the cup of liquid, and combine with this cooperative cause to make the reality of water, nectar, or blood. Discuss this with other Dharma students and slowly, slowly, you will understand.

In other words, all three perceptions are correct. Within this one object, the cup of liquid, we find the energy of water, the energy of nectar, and the energy of blood. It's the same when one woman looks at a man and sees him as handsome and another looks at him and sees him as ugly. If one hundred women look at him, there will be one hundred different views. Nevertheless, there exists within that one man the energy of what each woman sees, just as in the example of the liquid.

Another great Mahayana saint, Shantideva, explained Lord Buddha's *prajñaparamita* teachings—his teachings on the wisdom of emptiness—so that they could be more easily understood. He talked about how, in the hell realms, for example, a sentient being could end up in a burning iron house, surrounded by blazing fire, and think, "Where did all this come from?" Shantideva said that it comes from nowhere but that being's own mind. It's not as if someone in a place called Hell built that iron house, lit the blazing fire, and thought, "Aha! I am waiting for Thubten Yeshe. Soon he will die and come here. I'm ready for him!" It is not like that. Hell does not exist in that way.

The reality is that at the time of death, the powerful energy of the previous negative actions of that being, existing as imprints on his mind, is awakened, activated, and creates that being's experience of intense suffering, which we call Hell. Hell does not exist from its own side; the negative mind makes it up. Not only Shantideva says this. Lord Buddha states this in his sutras, and Shantideva refers to them. It is very interesting, and also important. Check up; think about it.

When you look in a merely intellectual way at the lamrim, you might think that hell is something real, existing from its own side, that there exists something concrete, built up. Then you think, "Oh, that's impossible!" and you doubt the existence of such things. However, Shantideva's explanation of the fires of hell and so forth makes it easy for Westerners to understand them. Your miserable view of reality is made up by your own mind, your own immorality; your blissful view of reality is made up by your own mind, your own virtue.

If you want to look more closely at reality, you can compare the psychological experiences of your dreams with your experiences when awake. What is the difference? Really, check up now. You always think concretely that they are different: "My dreams are not real but my daily life is really real."

If you check closely, you will see that this is not so: sometimes your dream-reality is even stronger than your daytime reality. Say, for example, you have a horrible dream. When you wake up in the morning, you feel so sad; it's unbelievable. You can't understand why. "It was a dream," you say. Hasn't this happened to you? You are intelligent enough to know that dreaming and waking are different, but the control this powerful dream has over you makes you uncomfortable. This shows that dreams are also reality.

Sometimes I dream I am eating delicious food, and in the morning my body, my nervous system, feels so comfortable; I have even gained energy. It is amazing. Maybe I am a hungry ghost! I'm joking. I am sure you have all had this kind of experience. This shows that dreams are also reality.

So the question is: What is reality? That's all. In all of Lord Buddha's teachings, with every important point he makes, he is saying that the mind is the principal producer of reality. Human goodness comes from the mind. Human problems, human badness, come from the mind. The pretas' hunger, the hell beings' horrible visions of fire—all these things come from the mind. Of course, good and bad exist, but only relatively. They exist only at the relative level, not ultimately. As I said before, psychological energy and various cooperative causes combine and transform into our vision of reality.

Here's another way of looking at it: How many universal phenomena are reality for you? You check up. In fact, not every phenomenon that exists is reality for you, is it? Our minds are limited, so what we perceive as reality is limited, even though universal phenomena are limitless. Do you understand? Energy that you have never contacted with your consciousness is not reality for you, but it is reality for others. Again, the question is: What is reality? This is another approach.

It is important to discover what reality is for your own mind, for your own point of view. Take a table, for example. You say, "I see this table exists." But actually, the table did not exist for you until you came along and looked at it. When you look, certain mental energy is thrown into this atmosphere, and then you say, "I see a table, this table. It is this and this and that." Although your dualistic mind perceives the table as something outside you, in fact, it is part of the nature of your mind; the table and your consciousness are unified. In the same way, it is your psychological energy that makes things appear good or bad. Everything we perceive is psychologically made up; nothing exists outwardly, fixed this way or that.

BUDDHISM IS NOT MERELY RELIGION

People think that Buddhism is only "religion." Actually, Lord Buddha explained his scientific ideas about atoms and the evolution of phenomena long before Western science did. When you study Buddhism, you do not study something that is merely religious, something to believe in; you study the whole universe. If you are fanatical, you're more narrow than expansive. That attitude is very dangerous; it produces anger and fear.

You should have enough sense to see the totality of the whole picture; you should have right discrimination. But it's difficult, because the Western scientific philosophical view actually teaches that, in reality, phenomena exist as self-entities. The Western scientific view is built upon that premise. Therefore, it's very hard when some lama suddenly comes out of the sky and says that what you believe to be real is not reality. "Wow," you think. "How can you say that? This is how I've seen reality since I was born."

Nevertheless, when you hear that reality isn't like you've always thought, your hallucinating mind experiences fear. But gradually, when you skillfully check up with wisdom, your conception changes, your feelings change, reality changes, emotions change, and discrimination changes. In other words, your whole universe changes.

WE LIVE IN OUR OWN WORLDS

Another way to put it is this: We all live in our own world. We say, "We're living at Chenrezig Institute," but in fact, each of the seventy of us here has a different idea, a different conception, of what Chenrezig Institute is. Therefore, each of us has different feelings, different emotions, different discrimination. It's in this sense that we're living in our own world. I'm not living in your world; you're not living in mine; but we're living together. We eat the same muesli for breakfast, the same rice and vegetables for lunch. We drink the same water. We do the same things—but still we all experience them differently. This is too much, but it is also so simple. If we all really were living in the same world, then when you laughed, I would, too, and when I laughed, so would you. But we don't, do we? So, you can see, we are all living in our own world.

Only when we all realize totality, the right view of emptiness, *shunyata,* can we say that we're all living in the same world, the same mandala. At that time, the conception of self-entity, self-existence—"I am this; that is that"— completely changes.

BECOMING AVALOKITESHVARA

It is very important that you understand reality in this way. Otherwise, when the lama says, "You become Avalokiteshvara," you will think, "How? Is he saying that my body becomes Avalokiteshvara? What?" If you don't understand that your entire world is created by your own mind, you will believe your concrete, sense perceptions and hold strongly to the view that something solid exists out there, separate from you. "This is real. That is real." And then it is difficult for you to understand how your wisdom energy can transform into the divine form of Avalokiteshvara. When you become Avalokiteshvara, it is not a fantasy.

Often Westerners question me about things. That is good. Really. I am happy when you do. I remember about four years ago, one of my students debated with me. He asked me a question that is perhaps silly, but is relevant to this point. He asked, "Just as you can become a buddha, can I become my shoes?" But that's entirely different. I hope you understand that.

Perhaps I should explain it again. When you become Avalokiteshvara, it is not your body that becomes Avalokiteshvara. Why? Because you are not your bones, your flesh, your skin. If you believe that only these are real, it will be difficult for you to become Avalokiteshvara.

What happens then? The psychological process when you meditate on emptiness is that all your conceptualizations of what you are, how you are, all your ego-projections, are dissolved; these appearances totally disappear from your consciousness. What remains is wisdom energy, and that wisdom is transformed into the divine, radiant light body of Avalokiteshvara. Another way of saying it is that you have a psychic wisdom body, a conscious mental body, like a rainbow body. It is not one that you can physically touch and say, "There it is," but it is perfectly, totally existent.

"Rainbow" reminds me of another example. Is a rainbow real or not? It exists, doesn't it? Yet, it is difficult to say a rainbow is real according to our ego's concrete point of view. When someone asks, "Is a rainbow real?" you say, "Oh..." or maybe, "Hmm...." Finally, you have to say, "Yes, it is real." Why all this hesitation? Because often we only consider something real if we can touch it. If we cannot touch it, cannot use it, we don't think of it as real.

Today, scientific technology has discovered many things that human beings cannot touch—energy, for example. This development of scientific higher consciousness is beautiful; we can carry it into our meditation. When people who study and practice Dharma examine developments in scientific technology, they can find extraordinary examples that they can use. This understanding of reality is very important.

MANTRA: RELATIVE AND ABSOLUTE

Tantrayana is sometimes also called *Mantrayana.* Generally, we understand mantra to be something we count or recite, but mantra is not necessarily just counting the sound. There is relative mantra and there is absolute mantra. Counting mantras such as *Om mani padme hum,* the mantra of Avalokiteshvara, is relative mantra. Absolute mantra is not this; it is the yoga tantra method, the tantric path of liberation. In other words, the path itself is mantra.

In Tibetan, the Sanskrit word *mantra* is *yigyurpa;* its connotation is roughly "mind liberation." Liberated from what? From ordinary conceptions. When you meditate using the yoga method of Chenrezig, Avalokiteshvara, your body is transformed into the divine form of Avalokiteshvara's white, radiant light body; your speech, into indestructible divine speech; and your mind, into divine wisdom, the divine consciousness of Avalokiteshvara. This method liberates you from mundane thought, from ordinary body, speech, and mind. This is the real function of mantra, of Tantrayana.

Let's say that even though you are not sick, a doctor tells you that you are. If you believe him, you will immediately feel ill. Yes? Do you understand what I mean? In the same way, if you believe you are a craving, ignorant sentient being, your ego will automatically respond in that way, and it will appear to you in that way. If, however, you transcend mundane actions and transform them into divine ones, they will become divine. That's what happens when you use the methods of tantric yoga.

KEEPING YOUR PRACTICE SUBDUED

Sometimes Tantrayana is also called secret mantra. Those who practice tantra should do so in a simple, subdued way, rather than make a big show of it. This is a very important point, emphasized especially in the Gelug tradition of Lama Je Tsongkhapa. For example, we don't permit the various personal things you use in your practice, such as your rosary, vajra and bell, tantric images, and so forth, to be shown to just anybody. You cannot make such esoteric things general in the way your mundane thought tries to make everything general.

When you keep your practice quiet in this way, it's not as if you're being miserly or trying to prevent others from knowing about these teachings. Tantra is very profound, and when you keep your practice simple and subdued, results will come; you will be successful. Making a big show of it causes distraction, and your practice remains superficial.

Tantra stresses that everything is perfect, blissful, and transcendent, rather than negative and difficult. With tantra, we get rid of this deluded attitude and transform such delusions into powerful blissful wisdom, which is the path of liberation. However, this can be a difficult idea to grasp. Suppose you say to someone who doesn't understand, "I'm not afraid of such and such a delusion. I can transform it into the path to liberation." The person would be shocked. "What kind of Lord Buddha's teaching is this?" they would ask. "It is impossible! Delusion is delusion. It is the opposite of the path to liberation, nirvana." Because you are learning skillful wisdom and method, you know it is possible, but instead of showing off, keep your practice to yourself as much as you can.

Sometimes people just think that they have powerful tantric methods and can transform poison into the path, that they are yogis or yoginis and can do anything. In fact, that's just ego. You have to be careful. Even if you have some power, you must be very careful about the effect you have on others.

RECEIVING THE TRANSMISSIONS
OF THE PRACTICE AND THE MANTRA

During this course, we should all try as much as possible to practice, to actualize. It is most worthwhile, and we are so fortunate. At first we will go through the text itself, *The Inseparability of the Spiritual Master and Avalokiteshvara*, moving slowly, slowly through the practice, doing the meditations as we go along. Each day, I will explain a little more, adding a new subject and going into details. In this way, the course becomes a meditation retreat.

Before we start practicing, in addition to the initiation you have already received, I have to give you the *lung* of this practice—its oral transmission, or blessing—by reading the text aloud.

Unless tantric methods passed on by one person to others have such a blessed generation, no Tibetan Buddhist tradition allows them. If somebody just takes a book from a library and reads it, there's not much blessing. A teaching needs personal contact to become real, and the reality of a practice doesn't come through words alone. The oral transmission is essential. It gives life to the teaching and keeps it alive. Otherwise, a teaching is simply dead.

Now I will recite the text. Simply listen; that's enough. It has already been translated into English, so I will recite just the Tibetan.

I will also give you the guru mantra contained in this practice. In this case, it is the guru, or name, mantra of his Holiness the Dalai Lama, as this text was written by His Holiness.

Visualize the syllable *Hrih* standing on a lotus at the heart of Guru Avalokiteshvara. Surrounding this are the letters of the mantra. Visualize another mantra emanating from this heart mantra, coming out through my mouth, entering your mouth, and sinking into your heart, where there is also a lotus. The letters of the mantra stand upright in a circle, clockwise around the edge of the lotus at your heart. Visualize this three times. The third time feel that the mantra at your heart becomes very powerful, indestructible. Now you are completely unified with Guru Avalokiteshvara.

Om ah guru vajradhara vagindra sumati shasana dhara samudra
shri bhadra sarva siddhi hum hum

This tantric yoga method of Chenrezig, Avalokiteshvara, belongs to kriya, or action, tantra, the first of the four levels of tantra. But just because it's not the highest level, you should not think that it is a minor thing and not so important. Actually, you could spend a lifetime investigating such a method; it is very profound. However, some time in the future, before we die, if we get the opportunity, we can also practice the highest yoga *(maha-anuttara)* tantra method of Avalokiteshvara.

PART TWO

Guru Yoga

Guru Avalokiteshvara in the aspect of His Holiness the Fourteenth Dalai Lama.

3 ~ Needing a Guide

Now I will talk a little about guru yoga. I will make it simple. Guru yoga is not something that comes only from Tibetan culture. It did not originate there and was not made up by Tibetan lamas. Guru yoga originated with Lord Buddha and was passed down from him through Manjushri and Maitreya, to Nagarjuna and other Indian mahasiddhas, and then to Tibetan gurus, down to this very teaching here.

The sadhana that we will practice here, *The Inseparability of the Spiritual Master and Avalokiteshvara*—from the beginning up to the point where we absorb Guru Avalokiteshvara into our heart chakra, and our body, speech, and mind become one with the body, speech, and mind of Guru Avalokiteshvara—is a practice of guru yoga.

QUALITIES OF THE GURU

The Sanskrit word *guru* literally means "heavy": heavy with knowledge-wisdom. The Tibetan equivalent is *lama*. The qualities of the guru are explained clean-clear in Mahayana Buddhism. If the guru is of poor quality, the quality of the student will be poor, too. We think this is a most important point. The guru should have at least the qualities of patience, wisdom, compassion, and subdued peace. If the guru is concerned with his own samsaric pleasure rather than the welfare of sentient beings, it is very dangerous. And anyway, in that case, he won't be able to help: if the guru is not practicing pure morality, it will be impossible for him to energize, or bless, his students and lead them into pure morality. Like dirty water, if the guru's body, speech, and mind are not clean, a clear reflection cannot be seen.

In the West, the idea of investigating the guru, checking up on his qualities, is difficult. You like excitement, new things, new flavors, and unless things are sort of dramatic, you easily get bored. You don't like to penetrate, to go beneath the surface, to investigate the reality of something or someone. This is a very important point; it is not a joke.

Let's say, for example, you are a tourist in Queensland and have no idea where to shop, what beach to go to, or where to have a good time. You need a guide, don't you? And you need to check carefully to find the right one. Perhaps you think there is something strange about the guide you are considering: "Maybe this man will take me to some deserted place; perhaps even destroy me!" You speculate this and that, and then tell him that you're sorry, you don't need him, thank you.

That kind of situation is nothing, actually. Nothing. You have already been in Queensland for countless lives—as a dog, a kangaroo, a bird, a cow. During countless lifetimes, you have experienced the Queensland environment, and still you need a guide. But going on a totally new path, a path on which you've never been before, never even dreamed of—the path to full awakening, to enlightenment—is something completely different. You must have a perfect guide, one you can trust. Otherwise, it will not only be very difficult but dangerous as well.

So you must have sense enough to check up, rather than be like, as we say in Tibet, a foolish man whose nature is like water. Water is not concrete, solid; it will flow in whatever direction you lead it. We shouldn't be like that. We also have a simpler example: When a dog sees liver, he does not hesitate; he gulps it down.

The relationship between guru and student should not be like that. You must be skeptical. It is important, isn't it? It is unbelievable how many religions, ideas, and philosophies there are in the world. At the beginning, you don't really know what is right and what is wrong, so you need to develop discriminating wisdom.

The qualifications I've mentioned so far—patience, compassion, wisdom—are the minimum qualifications necessary for a guru to guide students on the sutra path. As well as possessing these, a tantric guru should also understand the characteristics of the different deities and their mandalas and have received the initiations. It is rare to be qualified in this way. I am not qualified; therefore, I can give you only poor quality teachings. It's right for you to check up.

It's better to be skeptical and check rather than be too emotional and receptive and accept everything. It's not necessary to be so skeptical that you become agitated, but you should have enough sense to be able to discriminate between right and wrong, good quality and bad quality.

THE INSEPARABILITY OF THE GURU AND AVALOKITESHVARA

In the Hinayana, there is no such thing as guru yoga practice the way we actualize it here, as the unity of the guru and Avalokiteshvara. The Tibetan title of the text we are studying here is *Lama dang chenrezig jerme kyi neljor ngodrub kunjung shejawa,* which means "The Inseparability of the Guru and Avalokiteshvara: A Source of All Powerful Attainments." *Jerme,* translated here as inseparability, means unity, oneness. It means that apart from the guru, there is no compassion and wisdom of divine Avalokiteshvara.

Actually, Guru Avalokiteshvara—the inseparability of the guru and Avalokiteshvara—is the manifestation of Shakyamuni Buddha. You can say that. Before he passed away, Lord Buddha promised that his omnipresent consciousness of universal compassion and wisdom would continue through the vehicle of the guru.

By practicing guru yoga, by seeing the totally positive qualities of the guru, you can let your negative perceptions go. Most of the time your human mind thinks, "I'm a human being; I'm like this. He is also a human being; therefore, he must be like me." This is a misconception. By practicing guru yoga, you learn to understand that in reality, the guru is inseparable from the compassion and wisdom of Avalokiteshvara. And then you start to see the inseparability of these qualities and yourself.

Another way of saying this is that guru yoga practice gives you the inspiration to develop your own human potential. When you see someone with such positive energy, such compassion and wisdom, you are powerfully affected; you want to be like that, too. You have the same potential; you just need to activate it.

It's like when your friend buys a beautiful new car. When you see what a good time he is having, you are energized to get one as well. You can understand this, can't you? It's a good example. So definitely, when you encounter such powerful, good qualities as great compassion and wisdom and see the possibility of having an everlasting good time, you will definitely think, "Why not that, rather than confusion?" And not just for yourself, but to help all universal living beings.

We talk about unity, oneness, equality, impartiality, but we have to know how to achieve these qualities. How? Through guru yoga; that is the method. Guru yoga is extremely important. You should learn more about how to practice it and especially about the qualities of the guru. Many books on this subject are available, so you should study those, but it is especially important that you practice this text by His Holiness.

4 ~ Compassion: The Heart of the Path

THE TEXT BEGINS

> *To my spiritual master Avalokiteshvara,*
> *The full-moon-like essence of the buddhas' vast compassion*
> *And the radiant white nectar of their all-inspiring strength,*
>   *I pay my deep respect.*
> *I shall now disseminate to all other beings the standard practice*
>   *of this profound yoga.*
>
> *The root of every inspiration and powerful attainment lies solely*
> *with the spiritual master. As such he has been praised in both sutras*
> *and tantras more than once. He is of fundamental importance*
> *because the basis for achieving everlasting happiness is requesting*
> *him to teach the undistorted path. Thinking of him as being*
> *inseparable from the specific meditational deity with whom you feel*
> *a special affinity, you should visualize the two as one.*
>
> *The vitality of the Mahayana tradition comes from compassion,*
> *love, and the altruistic aspiration to attain enlightenment (bodhi-*
> *chitta) in order to effectively help all creatures become free from their*
> *suffering. Moreover, the importance of compassion is emphasized*
> *throughout all stages of development. Therefore, if you wish to com-*
> *bine Avalokiteshvara, the meditational deity of compassion, with*
> *your own root guru, first gather fine offerings in a suitable place.*
> *Sitting on a comfortable seat in an especially virtuous state of mind,*
> *take refuge, generate an enlightened motive of the awakening mind,*
> *and meditate on the four immeasurable thoughts.*

WHEN HE WAS ABOUT nineteen years old, after repeated requests from a disciple, His Holiness the Dalai Lama wrote this yoga method on the inseparability of himself and Avalokiteshvara. As you know, Tibetans believe that the Dalai Lama is the embodiment of Chenrezig, Avalokiteshvara, the buddha of compassion. Being the Dalai Lama is not the same as being the president of a country or some powerful ruler that people regard as a god. It is not at all like that. If you study His Holiness's biography, you will find how he came to be found and recognized as the Dalai Lama astonishing and beyond conception. Incredible things happened.

First, there is a short introduction, which starts with a praise to Guru Avalokiteshvara, *the full-moon-like essence* of all the buddhas' compassion. Full moon implies total, doesn't it? The compassion of all the supreme beings of the ten directions is collected, or manifested, in the divine form of Guru Avalokiteshvara, which is also the most blessed *amrita,* or nectar.

His Holiness then says that all realizations depend on the guru. (Lord Buddha explains this in both his sutra and tantra teachings.) With the understanding of the unity of one's guru with Avalokiteshvara, we pray to him to teach us the perfect unmistaken path. The root of all higher realizations is the guru.

Of course, as His Holiness implies, Avalokiteshvara is not the only buddha, or meditational deity. One can practice guru yoga with any buddha; there are many manifestations of guru and buddha to fit different sentient beings.

BODHICHITTA: THE HEART OF THE MAHAYANA

Next, His Holiness says that the real heart of the Mahayana is loving kindness and bodhichitta. This is what should be emphasized. He says they are important not just once or twice, but at the very start of the path, during the path, and right up to the end. Bodhichitta and loving kindness are emphasized at all stages of spiritual development.

Let's examine why they are so important at the beginning. If you don't have loving kindness and bodhichitta, you cannot develop the desire, the willingness, the enthusiastic wish, to begin to actualize the path to enlightenment for the sake of all mother sentient beings. Furthermore, the inspiration and strong energy necessary to then continuously actualize the path also come from loving kindness and bodhichitta.

We, however, are lazy. We sometimes sleep during meditation, don't we? The reason we're lazy is that we don't have enough compassion for others. If we truly wanted to help others, we'd always be busy, although not necessarily physically busy. But doing nothing with this precious human rebirth is such a waste of time. We don't have energy for meditation or for working for others because we don't understand that the potential for enlightenment exists equally in all universal living beings. When you understand this, you have confidence in yourself and much inspiration comes. You feel you are really something. And you *are*. Instead of always looking somewhere else for what is precious, realize that it is *your* being that is precious. *You* are the jewel.

Why are bodhichitta and loving kindness also important right up until we reach enlightenment? When you are successful in samsara, for example, you completely forget the suffering of other sentient beings. You enjoy yourself—sleeping, eating, and otherwise intoxicating your senses as much as you possibly can. You forget other sentient beings. This is the nature of attachment. However, when you reach enlightenment, buddhahood, you are filled with compassion for others. Such is the compassion of a buddha that he shakes with compassion for others; a buddha's manifestations number many thousands of millions, all in order to help universal living beings.

Earlier, I talked about nirvana. According to the Mahayana teachings, those who actualize tantric yoga are supposed to avoid nirvana. Say, for example, somebody says to you, "Okay, you have nothing to worry about. Just sit there doing absolutely nothing. I will give you everything, everything fantastic. You don't have to do anything; you don't have to help others. Or, on the other hand, although it is difficult, you can benefit others." Which would you choose? Would you choose to have a good time? Or would you choose to help others, even though it's difficult?

According to the Paramitayana and Tantrayana, to wish for nirvana, self-realization, is, comparatively speaking, a deluded attitude. Why? Because when you reach nirvana, you go completely beyond ego to peace and bliss. You become utterly intoxicated by the bliss of *samadhi.*

This is similar to a person who has been hungry for months suddenly being given delicious food and becoming completely intoxicated by it. This is natural. Those who achieve nirvana remain intoxicated by bliss for eons; they do not have enough loving kindness, enough great compassion.

Therefore, throughout the entire journey to enlightenment, the realization of bodhichitta is the most important thing.

REFUGE AND BODHICHITTA

Refuge

> *In the spiritual masters, I take refuge.*
> *In the Awakened One, I take refuge.*

In his Truth, I take refuge.
In the Spiritual Aspirants, I take refuge.

Generating Bodhichitta

In the Supreme Awakened One, his Truth, and the Spiritual
    Community,
I seek refuge until becoming enlightened.
By the merit from practicing giving and other perfections,
May I accomplish full awakening for the benefit of all.

The Four Immeasurable Thoughts

May all sentient beings possess happiness and the cause of happiness.
May all sentient beings be parted from suffering and the cause of
    suffering.
May all sentient beings never be parted from the happiness that has
    no suffering.
May all sentient beings abide in equanimity without attachment or
    aversion for near or far.

The text next says that if you wish to unify your root guru—the one who in the beginning put you on the right path—with Avalokiteshvara, you should first gather together offerings and arrange them nicely on your altar. Then, you should sit on a comfortable seat, with the back a little higher than the front, and with a special virtuous attitude, take refuge, generate the enlightened motivation, and recite the prayer of the four immeasurable thoughts. This is the preliminary meditation.

BLESSING THE GROUND

May the surface of the earth in every direction
Be stainless and pure, without roughness or fault,
As smooth as the palm of a child's soft hand
And as naturally polished as lapis lazuli.

Next comes the blessing or purification of the ground, the place where we are. Rather than seeing our environment as something heavy, or concrete, visualize it as Avalokiteshvara's paradise, his mandala, the manifestation of his divine wisdom-compassion, radiating light.

When we talk about paradise, the deity's holy mandala, we shouldn't think of it as existing physically, out there somewhere. It is the divine blissful wisdom and compassion of Avalokiteshvara himself manifesting as the mandala.

Take, for example, a park with glorious flowers all beautifully laid out. The person who designed it first thought, "Well, we'll put flowers here, something else there..." and so forth. Before it actually existed on the ground, the designer visualized it. So without thought, without the mind, where is this beautiful park? Where is anything?

Or, let's say you want to build a house. You go to an architect and say, "I have some ideas. Can you take them and design a house for me?" The architect then imagines everything, visualizes it; this is his projection. First, the house is in the architect's mind, and then it gradually takes on the reality of form.

It's the same here with the Avalokiteshvara mandala. If you understand the process, you can see that all the fantastic things within it are a manifestation of mental energy. Everything is a transformation of the energy of mind.

If you understand this, then when you visualize Avalokiteshvara's mandala, for example, your mind automatically becomes transcendent. As long as your perception of reality is one of beauty, that vision, that perspective, becomes your reality. Everything radiates. In this way, you can understand that this paradise, the deity's holy place, does not exist somewhere external. It is a manifestation of divine wisdom; it is pure energy transformed into beauty.

BLESSING THE OFFERINGS

May the material offerings of gods and humans,
Both those set before me and those visualized
Like a cloud of the peerless offerings of Samantabhadra,
Pervade and encompass the vastness of space.

Om namo bhagavate vajra sara pramardane tathagataya / arhate
samyak sambuddhaya / tadyatha / om vajre vajre / maha vajre /
maha teja vajre / maha vidya vajre / maha bodhichitta vajre / maha
bodhi mando pasam kramana vajre / sarva karma avarana visho
dhana vajre svaha

By the force of the truth of the Three Jewels of refuge,
By the firm inspiration from all bodhisattvas and buddhas,

> *By the power of the buddhas who have fully completed their*
> *collections of both good merit and insight,*
> *By the might of the void, inconceivable and pure,*
> *May all of these offerings be hereby transformed into their actual*
> *nature of voidness.*

Now we bless the various offerings. Making offerings is not just a tradition, a custom; nor is it just for the sake of beauty. It elevates you from your miserliness. Offering is a mental method to free you from bondage; it is the path to liberation.

Take, for example, the water in the offering bowls on the altar here. Sometimes Westerners think that offering water is silly. "I should offer chocolate," you think. "I feel so guilty. I eat chocolate all the time, and all I'm offering the Buddha is water." In fact, offering water is much better than offering chocolate, because when you offer chocolate, you're shaking with attachment. Your mind is not free.

Offering water is extremely useful. It has the quality of all jewels. Offering very clean water, without miserliness, is very powerful, especially when you bless it. Remember the story of the three beings looking at a cup of water? We see just water, but when we bless it and visualize it as blissful nectar in the nature of the divine, universal compassion of Avalokiteshvara, radiating light, that's what it becomes. Thus, every object—whatever appears to you, whatever exists—can give you a blissful rather than miserable experience. In this way, simply offering water becomes highly beneficial.

5 ~ Visualizing Guru Avalokiteshvara

In the space of the dharmakaya of great spontaneous bliss

THE NEXT PART of the sadhana concerns visualization of the guru, the spiritual master.

The Tibetan begins *dechen lhundrub chöku khaying*, all short, simple words, but the subject is profound. We could spend months, even years, explaining just this. However, I am sure we can condense the meaning a little. Refer to the sadhana as we go along.

De means joy, or bliss, and *chen* means great, so *dechen* means great bliss, great joy. *Lhundrub* means spontaneously existent, without causation, effortless. *Chöku* means truth body or, in Sanskrit, *dharmakaya*. *Khaying* means space, or sky.

You could say that this is a visualization of the evolutionary process of an enlightened being, the birth and development of a buddha. If you can understand this, you'll be able to understand your own evolution as well.

Earlier, I talked a little about emptiness. If you don't undestand this kind of reality, you will find it difficult to understand *dechen lhundrub*. Here, *dechen* and *lhundrub* are used as adjectives to describe the quality of the dharmakaya. The nature of the dharmakaya is everlasting, eternal joy, the greatest possible bliss, the final result—the unity of complete wisdom and complete method.

If you don't elevate your consciousness above relative, mundane thought, it will be impossible for you to experience transcendent bliss. When, however, you visualize the dharmakaya with an understanding of the nature of reality, emptiness, you will automatically experience bliss. The point is, in order to experience transcendent bliss, you have to comprehend, to actualize, the wisdom of emptiness. Then you can reach beyond ordinary conception, ordinary thought. It is possible.

If you are aware while actually looking at a beautiful lotus, for example, you will experience an awakening. When your senses connect with the flower, some energy is automatically activated within your mind, and you experience a good feeling. Experiment with this. When you're feeling a bit foggy and dull, look at a flower and see what happens. A joyful feeling arises automatically. This is completely natural, isn't it? Or, when a friend tells you about an enjoyable experience, you automatically get energized and excited just by hearing about it, don't you?

It is the same when visualizing Avalokiteshvara. When your mind creates a pure, divine vision, beyond ordinary conception, you are automatically elevated into a blissful space. It gives you a great deal of energy. You can discover this. Visualizing a deity leaves a deep impression on your mind, an imprint of everlasting freedom and joy. Automatically, all negative energy and defilements disappear from your mind, just as darkness disappears when you switch on a light. This has profound meaning.

Visualization is very powerful. It's a scientific process, not just something religious that you have to believe in. Don't believe in anything; just act and the result will come. That's all. However, since it takes intelligence and understanding to do this practice, those whose minds are strongly occupied with mundane thoughts will find it impossible, but those who understand the path to enlightenment, method and wisdom, can actualize it easily. There's no doubt about this.

Therefore, from the very beginning of your visualization, instead of visualizing substantial, material form—the view of ordinary conception—understand that Guru Avalokiteshvara is in the nature of the dharmakaya. He is the dharmakaya transformed into such a divine form. If you understand this, you will automatically have a transcendent experience.

THE ABSOLUTE NATURE OF THE DHARMAKAYA

Why does the dharmakaya have the nature of existing spontaneously, without effort, with neither beginning nor end? One explanation is that the dharmakaya is not subject to causes. This is made; that comes; this ends—it is not like that. The dharmakaya is fundamentally existent within all living beings. Fish and chickens have the absolute nature of dharmakaya as well. There is no difference between the absolute nature of a chicken's mind and the absolute nature of Avalokiteshvara. Only our dualistic minds see a difference: "Oh, dharmakaya is special; something absolute. My mind doesn't have that absolute nature." This is a misconception. The absolute nature of our own consciousness is already completely unified with that of the dharma-kaya. We simply need to recognize it, that's all.

The quality of the dharmakaya—absolute nature, Buddha, supreme consciousness, God, whatever—is exactly the same as the quality that exists in your own consciousness. At the moment, everything appears to us as dualistic, separate; but when our understanding deepens, the dharmakaya will appear in the mirror of our consciousness. It's a bit like television: the images are always there, but they appear to our consciousness only when we turn on the TV. The dharmakaya is like that: it is always there. You don't make the dharmakaya, but when you understand it, it appears. That's why we call it *lhundrub:* effortless, spontaneous. Actually, it is a very simple thing.

Let's say the sky is dark and cloudy, and your grasping mind thinks, "Oh, today is too bad. I want the sun to shine." If you have proper understanding, you realize that the fundamental nature of the sky never changes. Sunny or cloudy, the nature of the sky is there. The clouds are all so temporary; they don't change the fundamental nature of the sky.

Our delusions are like the clouds; they cannot alter the reality of our consciousness. It is always there. The delusions cover it temporarily, that's all. When you wear different clothes, your body does not change, does it? The reality of your body does not change when you change your clothes. The reality of your beauty does not change when you put on makeup, either. Your reality is always there whether you wear makeup or not, isn't it?

Creation, everything you are, is already within you. Nobody comes along and forcefully creates something on top of what you already are. Nor does your mind make up this reality. The absolute reality of your consciousness cannot change. Even though relatively you change, like clouds blown by the wind this way and that, the absolute quality of your mind, like space, is always there.

You can see that we need much purification in order to receive the vision of the clear-light dharmakaya. You have to make your consciousness as clear as possible; then the dharmakaya will appear. You don't need to grasp at it: "The dharmakaya is somewhere; I want to find it." No. It is there, always with you. You just need to see it, that's all.

Tantra gives the good example that the dharmakaya is like the sky and the divine form of Avalokiteshvara is like a rainbow. The space-like dharmakaya, which is formless and in the nature of bliss, transforms into the blissful, white, radiant light body of Avalokiteshvara, a rainbow body.

Westerners like rainbows—I've checked on this. When you see a rainbow, you are joyful. "Oh, there's a rainbow! Isn't it beautiful!" It has nothing to do with being religious, either. All universal sentient beings feel great enjoyment when their sense perception contacts a rainbow. This proves the power of visualization, doesn't it?

Whenever you visualize the blissful dharmakaya, your mind is incredibly energized, you experience deep satisfaction, and a powerful imprint is left on your consciousness. Each time you experience this satisfaction, the dissatisfaction that causes your misery vanishes. This is the method for cutting, or purifying, dissatisfaction.

When you make this method your own, you realize that satisfaction comes from the energy of your own mind. Because of this, it can go on forever, because it's not dependent on anything outside.

Most of the time, our pleasure and happiness are dependent upon transitory conditions such as the beach or chocolate. But the real chocolate, your blissful dharmakaya, is always there. It doesn't matter where you are—in the sky, on the earth, in the bathroom—it is always with you. Your mind is in the nature of the dharmakaya; the trouble is that it is covered, obscured. You look here, you look there, but you cannot find it. And when you are sad because you cannot find it, you think, "Maybe the lama will give me dharmakaya." But no one can give you dharmakaya. It is always with you; it is always with everyone. We just need to recognize it, that's all.

Therefore, we should prostrate to all universal living beings, because the absolute dharmakaya exists within them all.

THE PROTECTION OF THE BUDDHAS

In the midst of billowing clouds of magnificent offerings,
Upon a sparkling, jeweled throne supported by eight snow lions,

Next, there is a precious throne, which radiates light and is held up by snow lions. The snow lions signify the power of the realizations of the buddhas; they protect us from harm. Practicing a guru yoga method such as this protects us from harm by mischievous beings. In fact, the power of the wisdom of the guru can protect us from the vibration of the sun, the moon, the stars, water, the earth, everything.

This protection is significant. For example, certain sentient beings sometimes occupy, or possess, people and make them act in quite impossible ways. Does this happen in the West? Tibet has a long history of such things.

There are many reasons for these beings wanting to cause harm. Imagine, for example, that a married woman goes off with another man. Her husband is furious and only wants to harm her, but the circumstances are such that he cannot do it in this life. After he dies, he can be reborn as a powerful demon and enter and completely control her. Can you imagine? This kind of thing can happen.

Such a being is very dangerous and extremely difficult to control. There is no way you can escape because he is formless; any time he wants to enter, he can. Your body is almost his body. He completely shakes you. He speaks through you, makes you do whatever he wants. Day and night you suffer; you can't even sleep.

This is negative power and comes from incredible attachment. But it's not just his fault. We can't blame only him: "He is so bad." The possessed person also created the karma for this to happen. Karma is like this: if you don't touch fire, you will not get burned. I always use this example because it's an easy one. If you don't touch, there's no reaction. If you do, you create the cause for misery.

The snow lions, then, represent protection. They symbolize the power of the dharmakaya nature of the guru to protect us from mischievous forces and so forth.

THE UNION OF METHOD AND WISDOM

On a seat composed of a lotus in bloom, the sun and the moon,

On the throne are a lotus seat and cushions of sun and moon. The significance of the lotus is in the way it grows. They always need a muddy place for their roots, don't they? However, when the flower appears, its clean, pure beauty has nothing to do with mud.

This symbolizes the guru. He is the embodiment of the Buddha, and therefore, is not deluded. Because of our obscurations, however, we cannot communicate with the dharmakaya, so the guru manifests in the form of an ordinary, deluded human being. Like the lotus, which is born out of mud but uncontaminated by it, the guru is not muddied by the deluded human form.

Actually, we are all born from delusion, from mud. The energy of the twelve links of dependent arising—ignorance, karma, and so forth—forces us into these five aggregates. Nevertheless, it is possible for us to use our life in such a way that it becomes like a precious lotus flower, fantastically beautiful and completely beyond the mud of delusion.

The significance of the sun is wisdom, because sunlight automatically puri-
fies and relieves all darkness and shadows. It's the same when you have wisdom: you can purify all your darkness and limitations. Guru Avalokiteshvara
sitting on the sun cushion signifies that he has the full realization of wisdom.

The significance of the moon is method. In Sutrayana we say that method
refers to bodhichitta; in tantra it means great bliss. The moon on top of the
sun indicates unity rather than separation; it shows that Guru Avalokiteshvara has the realization of complete wisdom and complete method, together.

Sometimes we have method, sometimes wisdom; or no wisdom; or too
much wisdom but no method—our problem is that there's no integration.
The integration of wisdom and method is extremely important for human
development, even at ordinary levels. And of course, in Vajrayana, it is essential. In order to reach everlasting, peaceful enlightenment, we need simulta-
neous wisdom and method. This combination is the most difficult thing.

It's like good muesli: if something is missing, you think, "Oh dear, ordinary
muesli today." It is not easy to have everything—raisins, nuts, sesame seeds—
perfectly together. Well, in the East, it's not; in Australia it's easy! But you get
the point, don't you? Sometimes there's method, sometimes wisdom, but to
have them together, simultaneously, that's very difficult. And remember, unity
is not external; the coming together of wisdom and method is in your mind.

As I mentioned at the beginning, tantric art sometimes depicts a man and
a woman embracing. The male symbolizes method, the female symbolizes
wisdom, and their embracing, the union of method and wisdom. It doesn't
mean physical union; nor does it represent transitory enjoyment. It is psychological, transcendent, and an action of total purity.

Also, even though visualization is technically not what is meant here by
method, still, if you like, it is a method. And when you visualize, unless you
simultaneously have the wisdom that penetrates and understands the nature
of reality, your visualization can never become a powerful Vajrayana path.
Unity is what makes it powerful.

THE POWER OF COMPASSION

Sits supreme exalted Avalokiteshvara, great treasure of compassion

Here the Tibetan text says *nyingje terchen jigten wang. Nyingje* means compassion; *terchen* means great treasure—great treasure of compassion, as characterized by Avalokiteshvara. He is referred to as *pagchog jigten wang:*

distinguished, divine owner of the world. This is true, because if you actually have the power of universal compassion, of Avalokiteshvara, you can own the whole world; you can control the minds of all sentient beings.

Perhaps you think this is impossible. It is possible! I'm not talking about a power trip but about control in a real, positive manner. Think about it like this: since Chenrezig Institute started here in Queensland last year, I'm sure that more than a thousand students have already attended. These people have all received something here. Lord Buddha gave his methods and teachings a long time ago, and they have been passed down through generation after generation of teachers in unbroken lineages, right down to the lamas who have been here. Some of this power passes on to everybody, doesn't it? In other words, you have received some of Buddha's, or Avalokiteshvara's, power.

Therefore, if you really want to defeat an enemy, you should actualize true, universal compassion, the compassion of Avalokiteshvara. Then your enemy will become your subject, your possession; you will become his owner. I don't know what I'm saying, but perhaps you understand!

Remember when Lord Buddha was meditating, many mischievous beings armed with weapons appeared, trying to destroy him. Well, his weapon was true love, samadhi love. The power of his concentrated, universal love conquered the beings who were trying to harm him. Remember this. Then you will understand how it is possible for the universal, loving compassion of Avalokiteshvara to conquer the entire world.

Anyway, the whole world already depends on love, doesn't it? We all need love. You live for love. So you can see how you can interpret this as saying that Avalokiteshvara, who is universal compassion and love, has already conquered all mother sentient beings. In this way, we say that Avalokiteshvara is the owner of the world. It sounds simple, but check beyond the words and you will know more deeply what I mean. It will make more sense.

Nowadays, political people use loving words and appear to act kindly, but inside, their minds are full of quarreling. It's unbelievable. Actually, they derive their philosophy from higher thought, but they misuse it. Many people think such politicians are intelligent, but they steal divine ideas and employ them in a dirty way while saying, "I have this intelligent idea."

A good example of this is the way that communists talk about equality. They act as if they invented it. But equality is not their idea; it comes from Lord Buddha. Also, they try to force it: "You be equal or I'll kill you!" There is no way you can make people equal like that. With attachment, it's impossible. It's so transitory. Even if one day you managed to make everybody equal, the next day attachment would arise and people would be unequal once again. Look at the world situation and you'll see this clearly; you'll understand it perfectly.

Buddhism is simply looking at the world, observing the actions of human beings, and understanding what is going on. That's true, isn't it? You look, and you analyze: "That man is doing that, thinking this.... Those people are doing this and that; they are ambitious and violent, but what they are doing will lead them nowhere." We all do this, don't we? It is good to understand the human mind. And it is also good to know in what direction you yourself are going; otherwise, you won't know whether you are right or wrong and you'll remain in confusion.

Equality comes from the mind. From a mind that's free, equality comes automatically. It is impossible to create equality by force.

Suppose two dear friends should say to each other, "We are completely equal, and I especially want you to be happy. I want you to be happy even if I have to suffer." But when something really important comes up, the environment of equality disappears. The promise becomes empty words. If, in the face of reality, a choice must be made, you become more important than your dear friend. When the real test comes and you have to choose between winning and losing, you choose to win. So you can see, can't you, that unless you have discovered the reality of inner equality, your equality is meaningless; just so many intellectual words.

We often talk about loving kindness, but if we are not careful, if we don't understand the true meaning of love, we'll say, "I love you, I love you," but will not really be sincere because we will actually be wanting something for ourselves when we say it. Check up. In fact, we've been doing this for countless lives. We've been using artificial words and actions of loving kindness that have nothing to do with our real heart, our inner nature, cheating others and ourselves. It's one of the ways we tell lies. There are a hundred thousand ways to lie; this is one of them. So, you can see that it is extremely difficult to give true love to others.

True love starts within you. You can see this in people. At first, they are not so clear, but gradually, they begin to understand themselves better, to comprehend their own feelings and actions, and slowly they learn to take more responsibility for themselves. Thus, they gradually open up. First, truth opens within them; they have love and compassion for their own situation. Then, love and compassion naturally grow for others. This is true compassion. Actually, the process is very profound.

True love is unchanging, and the reason for true love never changes. Although you may change your color, your clothes, your environment, the reason is always there, always the same. But we use such illogical, transitory reasons for our usual love. "I love you because your skin is so beautiful." Maybe this is a silly example, but check up. It is like that. Skin is constantly changing, so your love is constantly changing. There's nothing solid there. The deep, underlying reason for love and compassion—our humanness, our fundamental equality—never changes, whatever the circumstances. This is not philosophy, fabrication, or mythology. Actually, it's science.

PURE MORALITY

Assuming the form of a monk wearing saffron-colored robes.

Avalokiteshvara—a precious treasure, in the nature of universal compassion, the distinguished owner of the universe, and in the nature of the dharmakaya—appears in the aspect of a venerable monk, wearing saffron-colored robes. This aspect indicates total purity; there is no vibration of impurity or mental disorder. And the saffron robe is not for decoration; it symbolizes the inner realization of renunciation, nonattachment.

I am also wearing a yellow robe, but perhaps it would be better to appear very ordinary, like Milarepa. However, since we're in Australia, if I looked like Milarepa you would probably think, "Ugh, look at that Himalayan man! He's in rags. Worse than our garbage bags!" However, the yellow robe symbolizes purity, nonattachment—although, of course, I have tremendous attachment.

O my Vajradhara master, kind in all three ways,

The Tibetan text reads here *tsawe lama sumden dorje dzin. Tsawe lama* means root guru. Your root guru, as I mentioned before, is the one who first showed you the essential path to liberation, who put you on the right path. This is the root; it's so simple. A beautiful flower grows from its root. Here, it's the same. Someone plants strong seeds inside you, and the result is a beautiful, joyful mind.

Sumden means having three, and refers to the three levels of ordination, or vows: Hinayana, bodhisattva, and tantric. The lama has these three, which means he keeps them purely. This is a very important point. If your guru does not have pure morality, it automatically reflects on you. Without pure morality, it is impossible to lead someone on a spiritual path, to elevate their mind to higher experiences.

The teachings are not just words. We receive some energy from the guru, some power that is beyond mere intellectual words. I think it is hard to understand this. It takes time. But through experience you can understand. In the Gelug tradition we especially emphasize purity, the morality of keeping vows.

Actually, purity is very simple. If you keep your body, speech, and mind pure, then you are pure, aren't you? You shouldn't worry about it, thinking that you have to give up all your things. It's not like that.

During a retreat or a meditation course, we try to create the conditions that make it easier for you to keep your body, speech, and mind pure. That's why we encourage students to keep the five precepts for the duration of the course or retreat. We want you to be happy and easygoing, to understand the teachings well. Such conditions give you more space to communicate. If you're a couple, for example, you meet your partner at lunch, and say, "Hi, how are you?" and in this kind of environment you can start to develop an even deeper love, rather than one that's merely superficial.

HOLY LOSANG TENZIN GYATSO

In the space of the dharmakaya is a precious throne held up by snow lions. Upon it, on lotus, sun, and moon, sits Guru Avalokiteshvara. Perhaps all this—thrones and lotuses and snow lions—seems a bit exaggerated to you; but if you understand it, it really is not. If you know the right way to look at something, it can appear differently and make sense to you. The throne, lotus, snow lions, sun, and moon are not substantial physical energy; they are all actually transformations of Guru Avalokiteshvara's divine wisdom. What you see is the reflection of divine wisdom.

The Tibetan reads *jetsun lozang tendzin gyatso pel. Jetsun* means divine; here, we can understand *lozang* as meaning wisdom. *Ten* means teaching; *dzin* means holding; in other words, holding the precious teaching, the wisdom, the teachings of Lord Buddha. It does not mean holding a book, a text. If you have wisdom, you're holding it, aren't you? It doesn't matter what aspect you show—white, red, or yellow, monk or lay person—if you have wisdom, you are holding, or keeping, the teachings. *Gyatso* means ocean and *pel* means magnificent: magnificent ocean. As you know, Losang Tenzin Gyatso is the name of His Holiness.

Endowed with a glowing fair complexion and a radiant smiling face,

Guru Avalokiteshvara's face is white and has a red vibration, which implies that it's radiant, or glowing. The white symbolizes kundalini energy and the red, the functioning of this bliss. His face is very loving, and his eyes, looking into the distance, are long, not wide open. This is significant. The eyes of those who are liberated and peaceful are long and narrow, whereas the eyes of those who are psychologically disturbed and neurotic are not like that. Lord Buddha is normally depicted this way, with his eyes long and narrow, signifying that he has reached beyond dualistic conceptions and sees the reality of emptiness.

Your right hand at your heart in a gesture expounding Dharma
Holds the stem of one white lotus that supports a book and sword;
Your left hand resting in meditative pose holds a thousand-spoked
wheel.

Guru Avalokiteshvara's right hand is at his heart in the gesture of giving Dharma, in the *dharmachakra* mudra—the mudra of turning the wheel of Dharma. His right hand holds a white lotus, and resting on its petals is a prajñaparamita text containing Lord Buddha's teachings on the perfection of wisdom. Standing upright on the text is a sword, which symbolizes the knowledge-wisdom of all the past, present, and future buddhas. Fire radiates from the tip of the sword, automatically burning and purifying all negative energy.

Guru Avalokiteshvara's left hand is palm upward in his lap, in the samadhi mudra, the gesture of contemplation. These two mudras together—giving teachings and contemplation—signify that he is an enlightened being, one who has reached beyond dualistic mind and can therefore simultaneously engage in the relative world—by giving teachings, for example—while remaining in complete samadhi. Not only is this possible, but it is how it should be: all actions should be done with perfect single-pointed concentration. But we ordinary sentient beings are limited. Our actions are separate from samadhi. We may meditate for a while, but as soon as we step outside, we lose our concentration.

In the palm of Guru Avalokiteshvara's left hand a Dharma wheel, a *dharmachakra*, stands upright.

> *You are clothed in the three saffron robes of a monk*
> *And are crowned with the pointed golden hat of a pandit.*

It's not necessary to say much about Guru Avalokiteshvara's clothes; it is not so important here. I mentioned already that the saffron robes signify purity; the pointed hat symbolizes sharp, penetrative wisdom.

> *Your aggregates, sensory spheres, senses, and objects, as well as your*
>   *limbs,*
> *Are a mandala complete with the five buddhas and their consorts,*
> *Male and female bodhisattvas, and the wrathful protectors.*

This part is a bit more difficult. Basically, we are made up of the five aggregates—form, feeling, discrimination, compositional factors, and consciousness—the four elements, the senses, and so forth. All these aspects of Guru Avalokiteshvara, plus his limbs, are said to be a mandala of the lords of the five buddha families and their consorts, male and female bodhisattvas, and wrathful protectors. This is a description of the extraordinary qualities of Guru Avalokiteshvara's body.

There are outer, inner, and secret qualities; what is described here refers to Guru Avalokiteshvara's inner qualities, but I will not explain all this in detail here. In general, this signifies that the aggregates, senses, and so forth of Guru Avalokiteshvara are completely pure and are in the nature of the five buddhas and the other holy beings. Visualizing in this way helps you understand your own pure nature as well.

Hinayana Buddhism says that when we die, having achieved liberation from suffering, *nirvana,* we disappear; our body and our mind both cease to exist. According to the Mahayana, it is not like that. When we reach tathagatahood, full enlightenment, the essence of our impure aggregates, senses, and so forth is completely purified, transformed. At present, we are related to delusion, but through the practice of tantra we can purify our mind and body, achieve pure buddha consciousness and, out of this dharmakaya, manifest in the pure form of a buddha.

We can refer to this pure energy of mind and body as Vairochana, one of the lords of the five buddha families. Sometimes you can visualize the guru's pure aggregates in the form of the radiant white body of Vairochana, but here we visualize Vairochana at the crown chakra of Guru Avalokiteshvara. We can visualize the other four lords at the other chakras: at the throat, red

Amitabha; at the heart, blue Akshobhya; at the navel, yellow Ratnasambhava; and at the secret chakra, green Amoghasiddhi. Each of these buddhas has his own mudras and so forth, but we don't need to demonstrate them here.

> *Encircled by a halo of five brilliant colors,*
> *My guru is seated in full vajra posture,*
> *Sending forth a network of cloud-like self-emanations*
> *To tame the minds of all sentient beings.*

Guru Avalokiteshvara sits in the vajra position, surrounded by rainbow light, which actually comes from his five chakras, where the lords of the families are, each radiating his own color. Guru Avalokiteshvara is simultaneously in samadhi and showing the aspect of teaching, and billions and billions of aspects of himself emanate from his heart. Clouds of these self-emanations fill the universe to lead mother sentient beings to enlightenment; it is beyond our imagination.

> *Within his heart sits Avalokiteshvara, a wisdom-being,*
> *With one face and four arms.*
> *His upper two hands are placed together,*
> *His lower two hands hold a crystal rosary and white lotus.*
> *He is adorned with jeweled ornaments and heavenly raiment.*
> *Over his left shoulder, an antelope skin is draped,*
> *And cross-legged he is seated on a silver moon and lotus.*
> *The white syllable* Hrih, *a concentration-being, at his heart,*
> *Emits brilliant colored light in all the ten directions.*
>
> *On my masters' brow is a white* Om,
> *At his throat a red* Ah,
> *At his heart a blue* Hum *from which many lights shine out in*
> *   myriad directions,*
> *Inviting the Three Jewels of refuge to dissolve into him,*
> *Transforming him into the collected essence of the objects of refuge.*

At Guru Avalokiteshvara's heart is the wisdom-being, *yeshe sempa*. This is Avalokiteshvara himself. He is white, sits on a white lotus and a moon cushion and has one face and four arms. Two hands are together at the heart, signifying total unity, and the other two are held aloft, the left holding a crystal rosary and the right a precious lotus. An antelope skin is draped over his left shoulder, which symbolizes bodhichitta. At his heart is a white syllable *Hrih,* the concentration-being, from which colored light radiates out into all directions.

Also at the heart chakra of Guru Avalokiteshvara is the blue syllable *Hum.* At his throat is a red *Ah*, and at his crown, a white *Om.* From the blue *Hum* much light radiates out into space to all the billions of solar systems in the ten directions, invoking all the supreme beings to come to him and sink into his heart. Guru Avalokiteshvara is now totally one with all the collected energy of all the supreme beings—similar to the way that Christians say that God is everything.

| *Hrih* | *Om* | *Ah* | *Hum* |

6 ~ *Making Offerings and Requests*

The Seven-limb Prayer

Prostrating

> *Your liberating body is fully adorned with all the signs of a buddha;*
> *Your melodious speech, complete with all sixty rhythms, flows*
>   *without hesitation;*
> *Your vast, profound mind filled with wisdom and compassion is*
>   *beyond all conception;*
> *I prostrate to the wheel of these three secret adornments of your body,*
>   *speech, and mind.*

Now we make prostrations and offer praise to Guru Avalokiteshvara. By seeing his body we are energized and filled with bliss. We praise his indestructible speech, which shows us reality and compels us to listen. And we praise his divine mind, his universal compassion and understanding. His omnipresent mind is beyond description, beyond measurement; our limited mind cannot measure such limitless energy. To our knowledge of his body, speech, and mind we make prostrations.

Offerings

> *Material offerings of my own and those of others,*
> *The actual objects and those that I visualize,*
> *Body and wealth and all virtues amassed throughout the three times,*
> *I offer to you upon visualized oceans of clouds like Samantabhadra's*
>   *offerings.*

Next we make offerings. We offer things that have an owner and things that do not. This means that we put our own offerings on the altar for Guru Avalokiteshvara, and we make imaginary offerings as well, things that we visualize. We also offer our body, our possessions, and our merits, or virtues, of the past, present, and future, all manifested as blissful, magnificent energy.

Confession

> *My mind being oppressed by the stifling darkness of ignorance,*
> *I have done many wrongs against reason and vows.*
> *Whatever mistakes I have made in the past,*
> *With a deep sense of regret I pledge never to repeat them,*
> *And without reservation I confess everything to you.*

In other words, we are saying, "Because my mind is completely covered by a thick fog of ignorance, I am unable to keep my body, speech, and mind pure, and all my actions are defiled. Understanding the results of these actions, I confess them all to Guru Avalokiteshvara and make the determination that from now on I will never do them again."

Meditating on emptiness, understanding the nature of reality, is the real, the perfect confession. When we do something negative, we naturally feel guilty. It doesn't matter whether someone says you are guilty or whether you are even guilty at all, you still feel guilty; psychologically, it just happens. This is our nature. When we meditate on emptiness, however, our guilt is automatically released and purified; we let go.

Rejoicing

> *From the depths of my heart,*
> *I rejoice in the enlightened deeds of the sublime masters*
> *And in the virtuous actions of past, present, and future*
> *Performed by me and all others as well,*
> *And by ordinary and exalted beings of the three sacred traditions.*

From our heart, not just hypocritically, we rejoice in all the actions of the divine gurus, in all our own positive actions of past, present, and future, and in all the virtuous actions of both ordinary and distinguished living beings—that is, the practitioners of the three vehicles: Hinayana, Paramitayana, and Vajrayana.

Rejoicing is very important. It has many advantages, so you should take advantage of it because otherwise, you become jealous, and that is not good. The jealous mind produces many psychological problems. Sentient beings are very strange. When your friend is having a good time and getting many good things, you really notice, don't you? You watch what's happening very carefully and feel jealous. This is common.

Even meditators feel jealous. Your friend says that he had such a good meditation, and you feel, "Wow! He is a new man: he has done only one meditation course and already has good meditations. I have done three courses and I have never had a good meditation!" You feel that you are terrible, which, of course, is not true. But jealousy is also there, isn't it? You're so jealous.

Rejoicing in the good experiences of others is very important. You can discover this; it is not just a custom. Lama Tsongkhapa put strong emphasis on this practice. There is a good example in the lamrim: A rich benefactor came to a monastery with an offering equivalent to thousands of dollars. In the temple sat a beggar who had nothing. When he saw the rich man make the offerings, he rejoiced with all his heart: "What this rich man is doing is wonderful. I'm so poor. I wish I were rich so that I could make such offerings." At the end of the ceremony, when the abbot, who was obviously clairvoyant, did the dedication of merit, he emphasized the beggar's merits, the virtue created in his mind by rejoicing, rather than the merit created by the benefactor. Why? Because the benefactor was proud and wanted people to think that he had done a fantastic thing. He came with expectations and ended up with nothing. The beggar, on the other hand, came with nothing and ended up with incredible merit and with the dedication.

Jealousy is an extremely painful mind; jealousy makes you restless and tired. On the other hand, rejoicing brings you joy. When you rejoice, you remove the painful nail of jealousy from your heart and experience peace and calm.

At Christmastime, for example, when you are all sitting around the table and everyone is giving and receiving presents, you might notice that someone else gets something special and feel jealous: "Oh, I wish I'd gotten that!" It's so uncomfortable, isn't it? Maybe your mind even becomes so unhappy and restless that you can't sleep properly that night.

The text says that we should rejoice in the merit created by practitioners of the three vehicles. We might feel that this is just a Buddhist thing, but actually it's universal. We should not discriminate. If we check the mind of the person practicing a spiritual path—Christian, Buddhist, it doesn't matter—we can see which vehicle they are. Their mind is the vehicle, carrying them to their destination.

Here at this course, for example, there are seventy or so people, and each of you is at a different level. Some are Hinayana; some Paramitayana; some are actualizing Vajrayana. But just intellectualizing about it, saying, "I am this; he is that," does not mean anything. We must know the real meaning of vehicle, *yana*, and not discriminate by rejoicing only in the merits of Buddhists but not in those of shopkeepers or followers of other religions. That is not right. Many, many people create virtue.

We should rejoice as much as possible. Rejoicing is wisdom. It is a poor understanding of rejoicing to think that it simply means, "Oh, I am happy." There is no taste in that. Real rejoicing takes much intensive wisdom; it takes much energy. Rejoicing does not simply mean that you are happy.

Requesting the guru to teach

> *I request you to awaken every living being*
> *From the sleep of ordinary and instinctive defilements*
> *With the divine music of the Dharma's pure truth,*
> *Resounding with the melody of profoundness and peace*
> *And in accordance with the dispositions of your various disciples.*

Here we are requesting Guru Avalokiteshvara to awaken all mother sentient beings from delusion, both gross and subtle, with the wisdom of his teachings, by ringing his wisdom bell.

Entreating the guru to stay

> *I entreat you to set your feet firmly upon the indestructible vajra*
> *   throne*
> *In the indissoluble state of* E-vam
> *Until every sentient being gains the calm breath of joy in the state of*
> *   final realization,*
> *Unfettered by the extremes of worldliness and tranquil liberation.*

You can say that this is a prayer for Guru Avalokiteshvara's long life. We request him to remain indestructibly on the vajra throne, in the state of unity of bliss and wisdom—thusness, or in Sanskrit, *E-vam*—until all mother sentient beings have been led into the most blissful state of full enlightenment. This enlightenment is beyond the extremes of samsara and nirvana. We talked before about nirvana; how, according to the Mahayana, it is almost a delusion and should be avoided. Enlightenment is beyond that.

Dedication of merit

I dedicate fully my virtuous actions of all the three times
So that I may receive continuous care from a master
And attain full enlightenment for the benefit of all
Through accomplishing my prayers, the supreme deed of
*   Samantabhadra.*

Dedication is important. We pray that the merit from all our good actions of the past, present, and future stay inseparably with us: "I dedicate all this merit so that I may develop my mind for the sake of all mother sentient beings and lead them all to enlightenment."

OFFERING A MANDALA

By the virtue of offering to you, assembly of buddhas visualized
*   before me,*
This mandala built on a base resplendent with flowers, saffron
*   water, and incense,*
Adorned with Mount Meru and the four continents, as well as the
*   sun and the moon,*
May all sentient beings share in its boundless effects.

This offering I make of a precious jeweled mandala,
Together with other pure offerings and wealth
And the virtues we have collected throughout the three times
With our body, speech, and mind.

O my masters, my yidams, and the Three Precious Jewels.
I offer all to you with unwavering faith.
Accepting these out of your boundless compassion,
Send forth to me waves of inspiring strength.

Om idam guru ratna mandalakam niryatayami

I don't need to explain the mandala offering here; there are many commentaries elsewhere.

BLESSING FROM GURU AVALOKITESHVARA

> *From the* Hrih *in the heart of Avalokiteshvara*
> *Seated in the heart of my venerable master*
> *Flow streams of nectar and rays of five colors*
> *Penetrating the crown of my head,*
> *Eliminating all obstructions and endowing me with both*
> *Common and exclusive powerful attainments.*

Now we do a meditation while reciting the guru mantra. From the *Hrih* at the heart of Avalokiteshvara in the heart of the lama, much blissful rainbow light radiates and enters your central channel through the crown of your head, completely filling you. You are purified of all defilements and gain all realizations. Visualizing this, recite Guru Avalokiteshvara's mantra as many times as possible.

> *Om ah guru vajradhara vagindra sumati shasana dhara samudra*
>   *shri bhadra sarva siddhi hum hum*

PRAYER OF THE GRADUATED PATH

> *Bestow on me your blessings to be devoted to my master*
> *With the purest thoughts and actions, gaining confidence that you,*
> *O compassionate holy master, are the basis of temporary and*
>   *everlasting bliss,*
> *For you elucidate the true path free from all deception*
> *And embody the totality of refuges past number.*
>
> *Bestow on me your blessings to live a life of Dharma*
> *Undistracted by the illusory preoccupations of this life,*
> *For well I know that these leisures and endowments*
> *Can never be surpassed by countless treasures of vast wealth,*
> *And that this precious form once attained cannot endure,*
> *For at any moment of time it may easily be destroyed.*
>
> *Bestow on me your blessings to cease actions of nonvirtue*
> *And accomplish wholesome deeds, by being always mindful*
> *Of the causes and effects from kind and harmful acts,*

While revering the Three Precious Jewels as the ultimate source
of refuge
And most trustworthy protection from the unendurable fears of
unfortunate rebirth states.

Bestow on me your blessings to practice the three higher trainings,
Motivated by firm renunciation gained from the clear
comprehension
That even the prosperity of the lord of the devas
Is merely a deception, like a siren's alluring spell.

Bestow on me your blessings to master the oceans of practice,
Cultivating immediately the supreme enlightened motivation,
By reflecting on the predicament of all mother sentient beings,
Who have nourished me with kindness from beginningless time
And now are tortured while ensnared within one extreme or other,
Either on the wheel of suffering or in tranquil liberation.

Bestow on me your blessings to generate the yoga
Combining mental quiescence with penetrative insight,
In which the hundred-thousand-fold splendor of voidness, forever
free from both extremes,
Reflects without obstruction in the clear mirror of the immutable
meditation.

Bestow on me your blessings to observe in strict accordance
All the vows and words of honor that form the root of powerful
attainments,
Having entered through the gate of the extremely profound tantra
By the kindness of my all-proficient guru.

Bestow on me your blessings to attain within this lifetime
The blissful mahamudra of the union of body and wisdom,
Through severing completely my all-creating karmic energy
With wisdom's sharp sword of the nonduality of bliss and emptiness.

This meditation on the graduated path to liberation doesn't need any commentary since there are many lamrim teachings available elsewhere.

This prayer is short, just a few verses, but it contains all the points of the path, right up to tantra. Meditate on just one verse per session rather than the entire prayer every time, and gradually you will get the whole picture.

I think this is enough for now. Try to see that the absolute reality of the dharmakaya exists in all living beings, including you. Meditate on this. Thank you very much.

7~ Merging with Guru Avalokiteshvara

My supreme master, requested in this way,
Now blissfully descends through the crown of my head
And dissolves in the indestructible point
At the center of my eight-petaled heart.

NOW VISUALIZE that the snow lions, throne, lotus, sun, and moon each in turn dissolve in light into the body of Guru Avalokiteshvara. Then Guru Avalokiteshvara comes to the crown of your head, sinks into you through your central channel, descends to your heart chakra, and completely unifies with your mind.

There's no need to feel uncomfortable: "Guru Avalokiteshvara is too big. How can he come into me?" He is in the nature of the dharmakaya—conscious, psychic energy—not substantial. If you understand this, your visualization will be simple; if not, your meditation is in trouble.

> *Now my master re-emerges on a moon and lotus.*
> *In his heart sits Avalokiteshvara, within whose heart is the letter* Hrih
> *Encircled by a rosary of the six-syllable mantra, the source from*
>   *which streams of nectar flow,*
> *Eliminating all obstacles and every disease*
> *And expanding my knowledge of the scriptural and insight teachings*
>   *of the Buddha.*
> *Thus, I receive the entire blessings of the victorious ones and their*
>   *children,*
>
> *And radiant lights again shine forth*
> *To cleanse away defects from all beings and their environment.*
> *In this way, I attain the supreme yogic state,*
> *Transforming every appearance, sound, and thought*

Into the three secret ways of the exalted ones.

Guru Avalokiteshvara completely unifies with your mind, then instantly reappears, sitting on lotus, sun, and moon, but this time in your heart chakra. At his heart is Avalokiteshvara, and at Avalokiteshvara's heart is the syllable *Hrih* surrounded by the six-syllable mantra, *Om mani padme hum,* standing upright on a moon disc.

RECITING "OM MANI PADME HUM"

Now recite the six-syllable mantra for as long as you wish. While reciting, visualize much blissful nectar coming from the syllable and the mantra at Avalokiteshvara's heart, filling your nervous system and purifying all your defilements. Feel that your Avalokiteshvara senses perceive all sounds as the mantra, all forms as Avalokiteshvara, and all thoughts, even superstitious ones, as the dharmakaya.

Simple or difficult? Difficult! Actually, this is just a simple visualization. Don't worry. You don't need too much detail; just visualize whatever is comfortable for you. The main thing is to have Guru Avalokiteshvara sink into you and for you to feel the unity, rather than a gap, or separation. Then, recite the mantra and visualize the purification. These are the important points.

PURIFYING WITH THE VAJRASATTVA MANTRA

When you have finished reciting *Om mani padme hum,* recite once the hundred-syllable purification mantra of Vajrasattva in order to purify any mistakes you have made while doing the practice:

> *Om vajrasattva samayam anupalaya, vajrasattva tvenopatishta,*
> *dridho me bhava, sutoshyo me bhava, suposhyo me bhava, anurakto*
> *me bhava, sarvasiddhim me prayacha, sarvakarma sucha me chittam*
> *shriyam kuru hum, ha ha ha ha hoh bhagavan sarva tathagata vajra*
> *ma me muncha, vajra bhava mahasamayasattva ah hum phat*

But first I will give you the oral transmission of the mantra. Visualize that the mantra comes three times from Guru Avalokiteshvara's heart, through his mouth into your mouth, and then into your heart, like electric energy being transmitted. The first one comes to sit, the syllables upright, around the edge of the moon disc at your Avalokiteshvara heart. Please repeat: *Om vajrasattva samayam anupalaya...*

The second time, the mantra comes from Guru Avalokiteshvara's heart, into your heart, sinking into the mantra letters on the moon disc: *Om vajrasattva samayam anupalaya...*

And the third time, again the mantra sinks into the mantra letters, unifying with your mind, becoming indestructible, like supreme, pure fire energy, burning up all the infinite lifetimes' collection of negativities, making it impossible for this contaminated, impure energy to enter your consciousness: *Om vajrasattva samayam anupalaya...*

The power of this mantra is incredible—it's even more powerful than an atomic bomb. We think that an atomic bomb has more power than we do, but that's exaggerating. I am joking! But I am serious, too. You'd be surprised. We should use this atomic energy against our delusions.

PART THREE
Mahamudra

8 ~ *Becoming the Mahamudra Deity*

UP TO NOW, there has been a short commentary on the guru yoga practice of Avalokiteshvara. Actually, the practice has many degrees, different levels. So far, I have explained it quite simply. Since you have been doing this Avalokiteshvara deity practice every day, you should now have some understanding of it.

The way we are teaching and practicing during this retreat is called *nyamtri*, or experiential teaching. It means we get an experience of the practice right now, that we're not so interested in intellectualizing. And usually, when something is taught this way, it is taught four times. The first time, you explain lots of detail, with more emphasis on intellectual information; the second time, you emphasize the intellectual a little less and put more emphasis on the practical; the third time, the practical is emphasized even more; and finally, you explain the very essence of the practice. This method of four different explanations gives students a good understanding of the practice.

Now I will go more deeply into how this method works, how by practicing the various technical meditations—how to absorb Guru Avalokiteshvara into oneself after reciting the prayer of the graduated path (see page 80), how to meditate on this unity, and then how to manifest oneself as the deity, recite the mantra, and so forth—we can be led to perfection, to the divine unity of Avalokiteshvarahood.

TRANSFORMING THE PLEASURE OF LOOKING

In the different levels of tantra one takes different levels of desire into the path to liberation (see chapter 2). In this kriya tantra practice of Avalokiteshvara, we transform into the path the desire produced by merely looking. Tibetan texts call this *lhamo la tawa chagpa lam. Lhamo* means deity; *tawa* means looking; *chagpa* means craving; and *lam* means path. All together, it means taking into the path the energy of craving produced by looking at the deity.

If you really understand the essence of Avalokiteshvara, every time you look at him, every time you visualize his divine, white, radiant light body, you will experience transcendent bliss. Automatically, bliss will arise. Even with ordinary objects, whenever there is attraction, automatically there is some sense pleasure, isn't there? But, as we all know, ordinary craving and desire make us restless. By practicing a transformational technique such as the yoga method of Avalokiteshvara with awareness and comprehension, the bliss we experience can bring integration and one-pointedness. That is why we say that tantra has the power to transform desire, that these methods allow us to take desire into the path. Of course, this does not mean that you can take any ordinary experience of desire and just imagine that it's the path to liberation. It is not like that.

When we visualize Avalokiteshvara, we should not see him as physical, as having substantial energy. We should understand that he is conscious energy, totally in the nature of transcendent, blissful, clear light wisdom and universal compassion. By recognizing this, your relationship with Avalokiteshvara completely changes; it becomes a transcendent relationship, a relationship of wisdom and awakening.

With this understanding, whatever bliss you experience automatically cuts through desire instead of producing it, which is what happens with ordinary sense pleasure. We often use the example of the insect who is born in a log of wood, who lives in it and at the same time consumes it. The insect comes from the wood yet simultaneously destroys it. It's the same with tantra: the blissful experience that is born from desire eventually destroys it.

This is a good, simple example. We can understand it intellectually. The technical meditations of tantra enable us to use bliss to release desire—to release all psychological problems, in fact. With skillful wisdom, it is possible to use a situation of desire instead of rejecting it. You mightn't like milk, for example, but rather than rejecting it, you can use it to produce fantastic, fresh cheese.

In order for our mind to go into the path, to be really usable so that we can experience bliss, we need much purification, many powerful blessings. Traditionally, we practice guru yoga for purification and blessings, and this is what we are doing here.

EVOLUTIONARY STAGE

Your transformation into Avalokiteshvara is technically known as the evolutionary, or generation, stage of tantric practice. But don't worry too much about the words. The whole process—the guru absorbing into and becoming oneness with you; the radiant light body becoming smaller, smaller, smaller, and eventually disappearing into emptiness; and then out of this emptiness, your becoming Avalokiteshvara—this is the essential method. This is the evolutionary stage.

However, our concrete conceptualizations about who and what we are prevent us from actualizing the deity. Our ego's projections are too strong. We have tremendous, concrete emotions—how can we release them? We cannot just say, "I am nothing, nothing, nothing." I could tell you all day long that you are nothing, nothing, but this doesn't make your ego-projections disappear. Do you understand what I mean? But with these techniques of mind training you can easily experience emptiness and thereby release your ego's fantasy, "I am this, that." Right at the beginning, we say, *tongpanyi gyi lha,* which means "emptiness deity." This is extremely important for actualizing Avalokiteshvara.

This sense of who we are is a complete hallucination. It has nothing whatsoever to do with reality, but it is so strong. When you had breakfast this morning, for example, there was such a concrete I enjoying it; a concrete I somewhere within your five aggregates; a hungry I in your stomach, perhaps. This is not an intellectual thing; it's completely instinctive.

Ego is very tricky. When you check intellectually, when you look for your ego, it disappears, but when you have strong contact with a sense object—such as attraction to or hate for somebody, or wanting your breakfast—your ego arises incredibly strongly. The rest of the time it remains obscured, in hiding.

Once you are able to actualize the emptiness deity, when you find yourself in such situations of strong contact with sense objects, you will be able to see clearly your concrete projection of "I," which is, in fact, completely nonexistent, opposite to the vision of emptiness. With intensive awareness, you will see the strongly hallucinated projection, which then disappears into nothingness. It is nothing, so it disappears. At that moment, you experience emptiness.

EMPTINESS DOESN'T DESTROY REALITY

The wisdom of emptiness does not destroy the reality of the external world. It destroys the mental fantasy hallucinated by ego and brings you an entirely different experience of reality.

When you realize the non-self-existence of the concrete projection of I—the idealistic fantasy that you have believed in for countless lives—it completely disappears into nothingness. Everything becomes empty. This experience is the wisdom of emptiness. What appears to you at that time is nothingness, not even the relative things you ordinarily see. When you re-emerge from your meditation and see forms, colors, and so forth, they appear to you as reflections in a mirror, but when you experience emptiness in meditation, there is no appearance at all.

When you first experience emptiness, it can scare you; you can feel as if you have completely disappeared. You can be sitting in meditation, experience emptiness, and suddenly feel, "Oh! I have gone completely!" Once Lama Tsongkhapa was teaching on emptiness when one of his students suddenly grabbed hold of himself; he thought he had disappeared. Lama Tsongkhapa was so happy. He saw that his student had just had an experience of emptiness. Such a precious student; his mind was ready. The moment Lama Tsongkhapa said the words, the student had a direct experience.

Thus, it is possible. This is a good example; it should energize you and give you confidence and encouragement. But don't be afraid if you experience fear in this way; don't pay attention to it. Just let go, but at the same time, be aware. Be conscious.

EMPTINESS IS NOT RELIGIOUS

Both the Paramitayana and Vajrayana emphasize emptiness. In fact, we say that emptiness is the heart of the Dharma. Emptiness is a blissful experience, like nectar. It is not a religious trip or just mythology; it is not merely something made up. Emptiness is scientific reality, not something simply to believe in. Emptiness is incredible; it is the heart of universal phenomena. When you realize emptiness, all concrete concepts of ego vanish. Automatically, you are liberated and experience everlasting bliss. Emptiness is the real Dharma; it is what elevates you to tathagatahood.

Emptiness is symbolized by a sword, whereas loving kindness is soft, like cotton; no matter how much you touch it, it never harms. The wisdom sword of emptiness, however, penetrates all obstacles and cuts through all delusion.

You can see how we hallucinate. This morning, your hungry I went to breakfast, and even though, as you were eating, the hungry I was disappearing, there was still the feeling of "I am a hungry person." You were still holding on: "Hungry me is eating." We have such permanent conceptions of ourselves.

We also think that yesterday's I is eating today's breakfast. That is also a wrong conception. Yesterday's you does not exist today. But this is how we think; we bring past experiences into the present all the time: "I am this, now doing that"—but it's impossible. The past is past. Even though the past has disappeared, you still keep bringing it with you. You don't want it to disappear, but it is nothingness.

Sentient beings are too much. We like to intellectualize about impermanence—"Everything is changing minute by minute"—but actually, we don't want to let go: yesterday's me is here today. However, whatever you have experienced in your life right up until this minute is not you. It has all gone. No matter how much you idealize, "I am this, I am that," it is all just conceptualization. The moment you identify yourself as something, you are already something else. Check up on this. It is scientific, not just something psychological.

A momentary experience of emptiness alone is not enough to cut through our concrete hallucinations, our fantasies of who we think we are. But an understanding of emptiness together with that experience—recognizing how we conceptualize our ego, how its nature is this and that, how we create the entire fantasy—really knocks the ego; something revolutionary happens.

Some people think that emptiness is a very difficult subject and that you have to study it for years and years before you can understand it. Of course, you can study it, and you must, but unless you really look at your hallucinated fantasy ego, the concrete conception created by your own mind, you won't get anywhere. It is not enough to have a merely intellectual understanding of emptiness. You'll still be hungry—like the tourist who hears all about Mount Everest but never gets to experience it. It is good to learn the philosophy, but you will really begin to experience emptiness only when you look, simply and practically, at your own ego's view.

When you are meditating on emptiness, for example, first there is a concrete sense of "I am this." Then, when you check up, when you analyze, suddenly this I disappears. When that experience comes, don't intellectualize; just let go without expectation. Again the fantasy comes, again skillfully check up, and when you apply intensive awareness, again the ego disappears. Concentrate on that emptiness, the lack of the I. Meditate on the object, emptiness.

Some Zen philosophers, for example, say that there is no object. But there is an object. It is not possible to have the subject, mind, without an object. Mind without an object is like an old man without a stick: it cannot stand.

Mind and object of mind are completely interdependent. You cannot say there is just nothingness. Mind cannot exist without an object; there is no such consciousness.

However, there are many different levels of objects, gross and subtle. At the subtlest level, you can *almost* say that there is no object, but there is an object. Emptiness, which is so subtle, is an object—not in the way we normally think of concrete objects, but in the sense of being something that the mind holds, or knows, that the mind meditates on. The mind cannot stand without an object.

Some people think that in dealing with emptiness it is good to block yourself off as much as possible from the objects that cause you to cling to self-existence, but that is not right. It's a bit like sleeping. We have been asleep for countless lives. Our eyes have been closed, and superstition just keeps going, constantly, like a clock; it is always there. Anyway, it is not our sense perceptions that cause us to grasp, it's our mental consciousness: the conceptualizations of our ego. Our senses are like the consul, but the ego is president. The consul passes on information—"I am this; I am that"—but it's the conceptions that are all-powerful.

MEDITATION 1
BECOMING THE MAHAMUDRA DEITY

Now let us do the practice.

I In the space in front of you there is a jeweled throne, held up by eight snow lions, that radiates light. On the throne, on a lotus and cushions of sun and moon, sits Avalokiteshvara in the aspect of a monk, wearing saffron-colored robes. Guru Avalokiteshvara's face is white and has a red vibration. His face is very loving, and his eyes are peaceful. His right hand is at his heart in the gesture of giving Dharma. It holds a white lotus, and resting on its petals is a prajñaparamita text containing Lord Buddha's teachings on the perfection of wisdom. Standing upright on the text is a sword, which symbolizes the knowledge-wisdom of all the past, present, and future buddhas. Fire radiates from the tip of the sword, burning up all our negative energy. Guru Avalokiteshvara's left hand is in his lap, palm upward in the samadhi mudra, the gesture of contemplation, holding an upright Dharma wheel. He sits in the vajra position, surrounded by rainbow light. He is simultaneously in samadhi and showing the aspect of teaching.

At his heart is the wisdom-being, Avalokiteshvara himself, sitting on a white lotus and a moon cushion. He is white, has one face and four arms. Two hands are together at his heart, signifying total unity, and the other two are held aloft, the left holding a crystal rosary and the right a lotus. An antelope skin is draped over his left shoulder, which symbolizes bodhichitta. At Avalokiteshvara's heart is a white syllable *Hrih*, the concentration-being.

Also at the heart of Guru Avalokiteshvara is a blue syllable *Hum*. At his throat is a red *Ah*, and at his crown, a white *Om*. From the *Hum*, much light radiates out into space to all the ten directions, invoking all the supreme beings to come to him and sink into his heart. Guru Avalokiteshvara is now totally one with all the collected energy of all the supreme beings.

2 Recite the Seven-limb Prayer, make a mandala offering, and recite the Prayer of the Graduated Path.

3 Now visualize that the radiant light throne absorbs into the lotus, the lotus into the sun and moon seats, and they absorb into the body of Guru Avalokiteshvara. Simultaneously from his crown downward and his feet upward, Guru Avalokiteshvara absorbs into the wisdom-being at his heart chakra, which, in turn, dissolves into radiant light.

This light, the transcendent supreme nature of Guru Avalokiteshvara, comes through your crown into your central channel to your heart. Feel complete unity, total oneness.

4 Now, your entire being and everything else magnetically dissolves into light, integrating into your heart chakra in the center of your chest. Everything gradually becomes smaller and smaller...atoms...neutrons...and eventually disappears into empty space. Experience nonduality, non-self-entity. As much as possible, stay in that empty space, seeing, contemplating everything with the right view of emptiness.

5 After some time, if you are sensitive, you will feel, "Now a relative vision is coming." There will be signs of this. Before the sun rises, there are indications that it's coming, aren't there? Now, in that very space from which you had disappeared, a moon disc, which symbolizes your consciousness, appears. Upon it stands a radiant seed syllable *Hrih*, a beam of light, filling all of space with light. With part of your mind, concentrate mindfully on this light, your own consciousness.

6 Now, from space, comes the sound *Om mani padme hum.* This acts as a cooperative cause for all the light to integrate back into the beam of light, the *Hrih*,
which suddenly transforms into the divine white, radiant light body of Avalokiteshvara. You, Avalokiteshvara, have one face and four arms: two hands
together at the heart signifying total unity and the other two held aloft, the left
holding a crystal rosary and the right a precious lotus. You sit in the vajra position on sun and moon discs on a white lotus. Over your left shoulder an antelope skin is draped. Everything is made of radiant light.

As you experience a clean-clear vision of yourself as the deity, simultaneously experience divine pride: "This is who I am." This is the practice of the
evolutionary stage.

This divine vision automatically releases your mundane view of yourself:
your deluded, guilty sense of self. You reach beyond your ego's idea. It becomes
a transcendent, blissful experience.

Don't intellectualize; just contemplate.

Having the emptiness deity experience—going through the process of dissolving into emptiness, the moon and seed syllable appearing, and becoming
the transcendent deity, Avalokiteshvara—is incredibly powerful. You should
try to actualize this. It has great meaning.

People sometimes worry that when they are looking at the deity, they are
simply looking at a projection of their mind, not the mind itself. However,
when you are looking at an object of your mind, you are, in fact, looking at
your mind itself. When you realize an object of mind in a clean-clear way, you
are realizing the nature of your own mind as well.

Remember, it's not only during formal sessions that you meditate on
emptiness. When you wake up, when you eat your lunch—you can experience emptiness any time. Ego is sneaky: when you are watching for it, it is not
noticeable, but when you relax and some situation arises, it sneaks out, so concrete. If you recognize your ego at that time, it will disappear. That experience is very powerful—and it is an emptiness experience.

9 ~ *The Profound and the Clear*

BEFORE LISTENING TO TEACHINGS, SEE YOURSELF AS THE DEITY

ACCORDING TO TRADITION, when listening to a commentary on a yoga method such as this, the student first meditates on the evolutionary stage practice, becoming the deity. Then, in each session, after reciting *Om mani padme hum* for three or four minutes, one does the absorption, dissolving completely into light and disappearing into non-self-entity.

Try it now: Everything is in the nature of emptiness. Then the moon disc appears in space, and on it appears your own mind in the form of the radiant beam of light. The light beam transforms into Avalokiteshvara's rainbow body. Contemplate on that clean-clear rainbow body...

In order to discover the unity of mahamudra body, mahamudra speech, and mahamudra mind, you should actualize gradually. Here we are trying to actualize the mahamudra deity Avalokiteshvara, who is in the nature of profundity, clarity, and blissful consciousness.

In Tibetan, we say *zhabsel nyime gyi ku. Zhab* means profound; *sel* means clarity, clear light nature; *nyi* means two and *me* is the negative, so *nyime* means nondual; and *ku* means divine body (*kaya* in Sanskrit). This shows the nature of the mahamudra body: your liberated wisdom energy itself transforms into the divine rainbow body of Avalokiteshvara.

A rainbow is insubstantial in nature, yet there is the clarity of its different colors. The radiant rainbow light body of Avalokiteshvara is like the morning sun embracing the whole earth: it radiates throughout the entire universe. The divine body of Avalokiteshvara is profound: it is in the nature of everlasting bliss, and its essence is universal compassion. It is transparent, like crystal, and it is nondual, because simultaneously you see yourself as the deity while perceiving the right view of non-self. Seeing yourself as the deity energizes within you great, blissful, transcendent wisdom and releases all mundane, dualistic thoughts. Avalokiteshvara's divine body is nondual, profound, and clear. This is the tantric yoga aspect of mahamudra.

THE UNION OF METHOD AND WISDOM

The great yogi Lama Tsongkhapa always emphasized, "The yogi who practices the Vajrayana path should actualize method and wisdom simultaneously, not one after the other." For this reason, the tantric yoga path is extremely quick: method and wisdom are experienced simultaneously, unified.

Wisdom and method are united when the experience of great bliss and intensive mindful wisdom are aware of the nondual nature, non-self, within the divine body. Within one intensive experience of wisdom, these two are perceived simultaneously, rather than one part of your mind seeing the blissful rainbow body and another part seeing the right view of nonduality. One experience of wisdom performs these two functions simultaneously.

MEMORY, MINDFULNESS

Thus, we actualize profundity and clarity, the nondual mahamudra. Our liberated wisdom energy is transformed into the divine rainbow body, which we contemplate. In the beginning, try not to see just parts of Avalokiteshvara's body—for example, just his face or his arms. Put your mind on the total object and feel unity. When you have a total picture, you are satisfied. Don't grasp, just let go as much as possible and keep your mind continually on the divine body of Avalokiteshvara.

Keeping continuity is what memory, or mindfulness, means. As long as you can maintain the energy of memory, your mind will stay on the object. Memory is like a hook and the unsubdued mind is like an elephant. If you try to hook an elephant too strongly, if you push too much, the elephant gets wilder. Therefore, memory should be neither too tight nor too loose; take the middle way.

In your development of contemplation, it is important to discover unity instead of allowing your mind to scatter. If you don't have continuity of memory, then during contemplation, when your mind goes to Melbourne or Sydney, you won't even realize it. When your memory is good, you can immediately bring your mind back to the object of meditation.

We say, "I want peace and happiness," but liberation—true peace and happiness—comes from contemplation. Lord Buddha taught many different ways of developing concentration, samadhi, and you can use anything—your breath, earth, air, fire, water, and so forth—as an object of concentration. In this practice, we contemplate the divine body of Avalokiteshvara.

MEDITATION 2
BECOMING THE MAHAMUDRA DEITY 2

I want you to try to experience what I have told you so far.

1 In the space in front of you appears Guru Avalokiteshvara in the aspect of a monk, sitting on a throne held up by snow lions. His face is very loving, his eyes peaceful. In his right hand he holds a white lotus in which rests the prajña-paramita and, above that, a blazing sword. His left hand in his lap is in the meditation mudra and holds a Dharma wheel. At his brow is a white *Om,* his throat a red *Ah,* and his heart a blue *Hum.* Also at his heart is Avalokiteshvara, the wisdom-being.

2 Recite the Seven-limb Prayer, make a mandala offering, and recite the Prayer of the Graduated Path.

3 Now absorb Guru Avalokiteshvara into your heart. Visualize that the radiant light throne absorbs into the lotus, the lotus into the sun and moon seats, and they absorb into the body of Guru Avalokiteshvara. Simultaneously from his crown downward and his feet upward, Guru Avalokiteshvara absorbs into the wisdom-being at his heart chakra, which, in turn, dissolves into radiant light.

4 Then visualize that everything you are—your entire nervous system, your imagination, your body and mind—melts into light. This light then gets smaller and smaller until eventually it disappears. Now try to experience unity, the view of emptiness. Have a vision of empty space. This experience is not actual emptiness, but by losing your conception of self, your picture of who you are, you automatically feel a kind of emptiness. That is enough; just let go.

5 Eventually, out of the empty space, a moon disc, which is your consciousness, appears. Contemplate that. Then, at the center of the moon appears a beam of light, the *Hrih.* It radiates light throughout universal space, purifying all the impurities of all mother sentient beings and making offerings to all supreme beings. You don't need to think this; it happens automatically. Then the light absorbs back into the *Hrih,* which is you.

6 In space, you hear the sound of the mantra, *Om mani padme hum.* This ener-gizes you—the beam of light—and you transform into the divine rainbow body of Avalokiteshvara. This is your own wisdom energy transforming into the mahamudra deity: white, four arms, sitting in the vajra posture on a white lotus. Your first two hands at your heart in the mudra of prayer, the second two held aloft holding crystal rosary and lotus. You see the crystal light body and simul-taneously experience bliss and nonduality. That body is your mind. Your mind is object, your mind is subject: the unity of wisdom and method. You are the mahamudra deity.

Experience satisfaction. Don't think, "I want to see this, I want to see that; the face, the eyes…" Just see totality. Contemplate continually, your memory neither too tight nor too loose.

Your contemplating mind is not separate from memory; they are one. Your wisdom is memory. Intellectually, we think there is the contemplating mind and then there is memory, but they are one.

10 ~ Clarity and Divine Pride

TWO KINDS OF MEDITATION

IN DEVELOPING perfect concentration on the mahamudra deity, we first need to develop an intellectual understanding. Then we meditate without intellect; we just let go. However, some meditators think, "The intellect is garbage; I should give it up," while others think that the intellect is more important than concentration. Actually, both attitudes are wrong. We need both intellectual understanding and samadhi.

With intellect alone, you can never experience emptiness, the mahamudra deity. Without letting go of intellect and going into contemplation, you will end up with your own fantasy rather than the real experience. However, when you start meditating, you need the intellect to put your mind into the right channel. Once it's there, you let go, without intellect, and the experience automatically comes.

The first step, during which you use the intellect, is called *che gom*—analytical meditation. *Gom* means meditation—penetrative, intensive analytical wisdom that clarifies the situation. This is explained in great detail in the lamrim teachings. Then, when everything is set up, you let go of intellectualization: this is called *jog gom*.

It's like driving a car. First you have to become familiar with everything—brakes, gears, steering wheel, and so forth—and then, when you are familiar, you can just let go and drive. If you try to drive without first becoming familiar with every aspect of driving, you will crash, but when you are clear, you can just drive spontaneously.

Meditation is similar. First, check up how much intellect you need before letting go into contemplation. Then you can be like the fish that just glides through water without disturbing it.

CLARITY AND DIVINE PRIDE

When concentrating on the mahamudra deity, you need two qualities: clarity and divine pride. In Tibetan, clarity is *selnang,* where *sel* means clear and *nang* means view. Clarity is the antidote to your ordinary vision and mundane thoughts, which are released automatically. When your view is clear and divine, you cannot be energized by the mundane view, and your restless mind is cut.

Divine pride—thinking, "I am the mahamudra deity"—is an antidote to the ordinary concepts of ego; it counters the psychological belief in the fantasy of your own identity. The Tibetan for pride is *ngagyel.*

At the moment, with respect to what we think we are, we're living in a fantasy world. It's completely imagined—like thinking there's an elephant in our bedroom. What we think we are has nothing whatsoever to do with reality. Hearing this might freak you out—"I know who I am!" But, according to Lord Buddha, our ego's way of putting together what we are is a total fantasy. We create this bubble of our own identity and then spend all our time running here and there trying to keep it together.

You can see the psychological effect of divine pride. When you feel that your liberated wisdom energy is the mahamudra deity Avalokiteshvara, there's no way you can be depressed; there's no room. There's no way an elephant can enter your bedroom, either.

When you meditate, first put energy into developing clarity: perceiving yourself very clearly as the mahamudra deity. Once you have confidence that your visualization is clear, generate divine pride.

If your divine pride is too strong and you lose clarity, adjust your meditation. Similarly, if you feel dissatisfied when you are concentrating, if you start thinking, "I need more clarity," and try too hard, you will become distracted. It's important to feel satisfied. Just put your mind on the object and let go. If you always want more, your mind will get distracted; there'll be too much excitement.

Be skillful—you need to know how much energy to put into clarity and divine pride. However, you will learn this from your own experience.

MEDITATION 3
CLARITY AND DIVINE PRIDE

This time, I want you to actualize clarity and divine pride. Remember that clarity is an antidote to our ordinary vision, to mundane thoughts, and divine pride is an antidote to the ordinary conception of the ego. Each has its own function.

Do not think that it is your flesh and bones that become Avalokiteshvara.

That's why I sometimes refer to our psychic body, our conscious body, or why I say that it's our liberated wisdom energy that is transformed into the divine Avalokiteshvara form. I use these different terms to help you understand the process.

You should think, "Yes, I have some liberated wisdom, especially when my concrete imagination, my conceptualization, of who I think I am disappears." Then you can experience emptiness to some extent. This is your wisdom, and it is this liberated wisdom that transforms into the mahamudra deity, Avalokiteshvara. "This is who I am."

Now let us do the meditation.

1 In the space in front of you is Guru Avalokiteshvara. He sits on a throne held up by snow lions and looks at you lovingly. At his heart is the wisdom-being, Avalokiteshvara himself.

2 Recite the Seven-limb Prayer, make a mandala offering, and recite the Prayer of the Graduated Path.

3 Now visualize that the throne melts into light and absorbs into Guru Avalokiteshvara's body. His radiant light body melts into the moon at his heart, simultaneously from the feet upward and the crown downward. Then the moon absorbs into the *Hrih* at its center, which becomes like an egg of radiant light. **This radiant light enters your central channel and descends to your heart chakra, the essence of Avalokiteshvara becoming one with you. The egg-light radiates throughout your entire nervous system.**

4 All the energy of your own body melts, dissolves, into radiant light. This light becomes smaller, smaller…atoms…neutrons…then disappears into empty space. Let go into nothingness, with one part of your mind understanding the right view of non-self-entity.

5 Now a precious lotus appears. On the lotus is a moon with a beam of light at its center. Concentrate on the beam of light. Feel unity with the beam of light; let your mind sink into it. Don't think, "Now I'm concentrating." Feel that your mind actually goes into that beam of light; don't feel that you are looking at it from the outside.

   Light radiates out from the beam to embrace all universal phenomena.

6 Then you hear the divine sound of *Om mani padme hum* coming from space, energizing, stimulating the light to absorb back into the beam at your heart. Your liberated wisdom energy beam of light instantly transforms into Avalokiteshvara.

See each part of yourself clearly: your divine, radiant light body, as clean and clear as crystal; your two hands holding the rosary and lotus; the other two hands at your heart; your eyes; the antelope skin draped over your left shoulder. Everything is clean-clear. Concentrate on this clarity.

Do not feel that you are looking at an object outside yourself, as if it were another person. Feel: "This blissful, nonduality rainbow body is me; this is who I am." This is divine pride.

8 Now change your concentration. At the heart of you, Avalokiteshvara, there is a radiant light moon and upon it a beam of light. Instantly, your Avalokiteshvara rainbow body dissolves into the moon, from the feet upward and the crown downward. The moon then dissolves into the beam of light. This becomes smaller, smaller...atoms...neutrons...and eventually disappears into empty space: experience nonduality, non-self-entity.

Now, in space, a beam of light appears on a moon, which transforms into Avalokiteshvara, which is yourself. See this clearly and at the same time experience the right view of emptiness. Experience this as if you were a magician who has conjured up, say, a horse: when ordinary people see it they think it is real, but the magician, who also sees it, knows that it is not.

In this way, experience the mahamudra deity.

11 ~ Transforming All Appearances into Avalokiteshvara

W E ARE EXPERIENCING this meditation course as an intensive retreat. During this retreat, we should actualize this yoga method all the time, day and night. As well as seeing yourself as the mahamudra deity, you should also try to see all sentient beings in that divine form. Moreover, you should not perceive your surroundings as mundane. As the transcendent mahamudra deity, you should not have the ordinary impression that we are sitting here in Queensland, Australia; that view is not right. You have to realize that everything is Avalokiteshvara's mandala and his mandala is a transformation of blissful wisdom.

MEDITATION 4
THE HALLUCINATED VISION DISSOLVES INTO LIGHT

1, 2, 3, 4 Guru Avalokiteshvara sits on a throne, a sun, and moon disc, in the aspect of a monk, with Avalokiteshvara at his heart. After reciting the prayers, Guru Avalokiteshvara absorbs into you, and you dissolve into emptiness. Contemplate each step.

5 When from space the moon disc and beam of light appear and the light goes out to embrace all universal energy, everything that the light embraces—all of Chenrezig Institute, all of Queensland, all of Australia, the whole world—dissolves, melts; all sentient beings, everything, melt into radiant light.

   Make sure you transform everything into light, especially whatever you're caught up in, whatever attracts you. Psychologically, this is incredibly effective. The entire puzzle-conflict environment is digested, magnetically absorbed into the radiant light, so now you can't have any concrete vision of real beaches or oceans or mountains. That hallucinated painting dissolves. You no longer have superstitious thoughts about what's going to come from the kitchen: "I wonder what they're going to give me for dinner?"

6 Then, after this strong absorption with strong, concentrated awareness, the beam of light is transformed into the Avalokiteshvara deity body. In the whole of universal space there is only you, Avalokiteshvara. Contemplate the clarity of this.

When distraction comes, recognize that it is superstitious mental energy. Instead of rejecting it, watch it, intensively, consciously—the bubble, the superstitious distraction, will disappear of its own accord.

THE REALITY OF OUR FANTASIES

Actually, you could say that when the distraction disappears into empty space, this is, in fact, the reality of the superstitious view. Let's say that someone tells you a big story that in Brisbane a spaceship has landed from the moon, and in that spaceship are moon people. They are as tall as the hill down there, their mouths are the size of Chenrezig gompa, and they have two conches in their hair. Well! You'd be very excited, hearing this, and would want to check it out for yourself. You'd rush down to Brisbane, asking for information about where to find the spaceship, searching here and there—but you wouldn't find anything. After that big story, all that excitement, all that seeking, you find nothing. At that moment there would be a feeling of space, wouldn't there? As if you'd lost your fantasy object. "I came all this way, and there's nothing." There'd be some sense of emptiness.

Of course, in that situation, you'd feel dissatisfied to find nothing, but actually, that finding of nothing is the reality of the fantasy, isn't it? After all that emotion and idealism, you end up finding nothing. That nothingness is the reality of the fantasy. Does this make sense? I am talking psychologically. Our ordinary experiences produce great dissatisfaction, but it's ridiculous. It's because we do not face reality. Our fantasies are not reality; therefore, when they arise and we check them out, we find nothing. But that is the reality of our fantasies.

When superstition arises during your samadhi meditation on the divine deity, don't reject it. Just look at it and it will disappear naturally; automatically, you will return to the meditation object. Sometimes, instead of looking at the superstition itself, you can look at the object of the superstitious thought. Check, watch—it, too, will naturally disappear.

THE THREE SECRET WAYS OF THE EXALTED ONES

There is another way of releasing distraction. Whatever distraction arises, transform it into the divine Avalokiteshvara body, the mahamudra deity, and allow it to sink into and unify with you, Avalokiteshvara. Recognize whatever appearance arises as the embodiment of the mahamudra deity, whatever sound arises as the transcendent mantra, and whatever thought arises as the dharmakaya of Avalokiteshvara.

The text mentions "the three secret ways of the exalted ones": "View all surroundings as a blissful abode, see all beings as manifestations of the deity, and hear all sound as mantra, intuitively knowing everything to be empty of true existence."

Why are the mahamudra deity's body, speech, and blissful wisdom called secret? Because at the moment, we are obscured; we can't see. They are not called secret because they're not supposed to be shown; the implication of secret is that they are difficult to realize.

Actually, the Buddhist scientific experience is that everything—form, color, smell, water, fire—has sound energy. Perhaps it is difficult for us to see that this pillar holding up the roof has sound! Has Western science explained this? Still, I think modern scientific experience and Lord Buddha's scientific experience are coming together.

Sound is so simple. Perhaps someone says to you, "You're very pretty"— this sound makes you happy. But when you hear someone else say, "You're ugly," this sound doesn't make you happy at all! One sound takes you up; the other brings you down. But it's just psychological, isn't it?

If you look at it another way, both statements are just sound, but we exaggerate their meaning and are emotionally shaken. We are like children; we have no wisdom, no control. It's common to find that after a meditation course such as this, when you go back into your usual environment, you are just like a child; you just follow whatever is there. You can't keep your own mandala together, and then you blame everybody else: society, your situation, your neighbors, your children, and so forth.

However, when you gain more understanding, sounds will bring only a liberated feeling; no matter what sounds arise, you'll hear them all as equal.

Meditation 5
Reciting the Mantra

First we will go through the stages of the meditation, then we can recite the mantra.

1 Visualize Guru Avalokiteshvara in the aspect of a monk, sitting on a throne held up by snow lions. At his heart is Avalokiteshvara.

2 Recite the Seven-limb Prayer, make a mandala offering, and recite the Prayer of the Graduated Path.

3 Now absorb Guru Avalokiteshvara into your heart. Visualize that the radiant light throne absorbs into the lotus, the lotus into the sun and moon seats, and they absorb into the body of Guru Avalokiteshvara. Simultaneously from his crown downward and his feet upward, Guru Avalokiteshvara absorbs into the wisdom-being at his heart chakra, which, in turn, dissolves into radiant light.

4 Then visualize that you melt into light. The light then gets smaller and smaller until eventually disappears. Experience unity, the view of emptiness. Have a vision of empty space.

5 Eventually, out of the empty space, a moon disc, which is your consciousness, appears. Contemplate that. Then, at the center of the moon appears a beam of light, the *Hrih*. It radiates light throughout universal space, purifying all the impurities of all mother sentient beings and making offerings to all supreme beings. Then the light absorbs back into the *Hrih,* which is you.

6 In space, you hear the sound of the mantra, *Om mani padme hum.* This energizes you—the beam of light—and you transform into the divine rainbow body of Avalokiteshvara. This is your own wisdom energy transforming into the mahamudra deity: white, four arms, sitting in the vajra posture on a white lotus. Your first two hands at your heart in the mudra of prayer, the second two held aloft holding crystal rosary and lotus. You see the crystal light body and simultaneously experience bliss and nonduality. That body is your mind. Your mind is object, your mind is subject: the unity of wisdom and method. You are the mahamudra deity.

7 When you feel that you can concentrate on the divine body as long as you wish, you'll be encouraged to move on to a more subtle concentration. At your Avalokiteshvara heart is the six-syllable mantra *Om mani padme hum*. Concentrate on the mantra as you recite it. Recite the mantra loud enough for you to hear it but not so loud that others can. Also, remember that the mantra, too, is the transformation of blissful wisdom.

　　While reciting the mantra, imagine light radiating from it throughout all universal space, transforming the energy of the universe into light, which sinks back into the mantra at your heart.

Actually, psychologically, there is a great deal of activity at your heart—more activity than in a supermarket. We often hear people say, "You should be open," but to open your heart, you need a key. There is a relationship between your psychological world and your nervous system. Therefore, it is very important to send light from your Avalokiteshvara heart and then to absorb everything back into it.

　　Currently, all the miserable, contaminated energy in your nervous system—attachment, anger, and the rest—is activated, preventing your pure energy from functioning. Dissolving everything into light and absorbing it into your Avalokiteshvara heart releases your blocked energy, dissolves it into your central channel, and energizes your pure energy, thereby allowing it to function. This is the key to opening your heart.

THE BODY IS IMPORTANT, TOO

Actually, tantric yoga emphasizes the physical as well as the psychological—both are important. You cannot say, "Oh, my rag body is no good, I don't care about it!" This is not right. In fact, certain initiations come with a vow that says you should never criticize your body but see it in a positive way, take care of it, and keep it clean and healthy.

　　Of course, the Hinayana part of the lamrim does talk about how the five aggregates are in the nature of suffering, and this is also correct. There is no contradiction between the Hinayana and the Vajrayana; it's a question of the individual's level of mind. All these teachings are a part of the graduated path to enlightenment. At the beginning we need a certain approach; then, when realizations come, we discard it and move on. According to tantric yoga, this body is very precious, like a diamond—we can use its energy on the blissful path to liberation.

Also, there are explanations about how each chakra has a different function. Let's say you have a difficult time experiencing bliss in your meditation. Your concentration might be good, but you find it difficult to experience bliss. What you can do in that case is bring the mantra down from the heart chakra to the navel, and concentrate on that. See if the feeling changes; see if you feel bliss. If that does not work, you can bring the mantra down even further, to the lower chakra, and contemplate the mantra there. That should automatically produce a blissful experience.

However, if you experience bliss without penetrative, intensive wisdom, the right view, your bliss becomes an ordinary state of mind. Therefore, when experiencing bliss, it is very important that you simultaneously have the recognition of emptiness. You need that energy in order to make your experience transcendent.

Actually, if you really understand the mahamudra body, the evolutionary stage, you don't need to do anything; bliss and emptiness naturally come together. The nature of the rainbow body is automatically blissful and clean-clear. Just seeing the divine Avalokiteshvara body completely energizes transcendent bliss in the same way that seeing a beautiful human body energizes blissful samsaric energy. Just seeing Avalokiteshvara's rainbow body brings an incredibly blissful experience and a feeling of unity, of non-self-entity. When you really understand this process, these things come together.

I think we can stop here now. Remember, when you are satisfied with your concentration on the mahamudra body, you can shift your concentration to the mantra.

And one more thing. When you see something bad, think, "Bad is not so bad," and when you see something fantastic, think, "Good is not so good." This might sound silly—"What do you mean, 'Bad is not bad…good is not good'?"—but actually, it is profound. When you have this kind of understanding, you will have more control and not be so influenced by everything around you.

12 ~ *Verbal and Mental Mantra*

PERHAPS YOU'RE THINKING, "How can I actualize such a profound practice, containing these universal subjects, all in one session!" Don't think like that. If you think it is too much, it will be difficult. Actually, when it's all put together, it's quite easy. Therefore, let's run through the entire practice from the beginning to end.

MEDITATION 6
TRANSFORM EVERYTHING INTO THE MANTRA

1 Visualize in front of you the inseparability of the guru and divine Avalokiteshvara, seated on a moon seat and lotus on a radiant throne. Don't think that you have put him there; instead, imagine that with his psychic ability he has come to you, in the space in front: "If you want me, look, here I am!"
  Om mani padme hum, Om mani padme hum, Om mani padme hum...

2 Recite the Seven-limb Prayer, make a mandala offering, and recite the Prayer of the Graduated Path.

3 The radiant light throne absorbs into the lotus, the lotus into the moon seat, the moon seat into the body of Guru Avalokiteshvara. From his crown downward and his feet upward, he absorbs into his heart chakra, becoming a radiant egg of light. This egg-light, the transcendent supreme nature of Guru Avalokiteshvara, comes through your crown into your central channel to your heart. Feel unity, oneness, with Guru Avalokiteshvara.

4 From the egg-light much radiant light fills all your nervous system. Your radiant light body absorbs from the feet upward and the crown downward, becoming smaller, smaller, smaller...atoms...neutrons...and eventually disappearing into empty space, infinite in nature. Your consciousness goes into empty

space, seeing the nature of totality, no beginning...no end...no self-entity....
Let go of your mind into nonduality....

5 Suddenly, out of infinite space, nonduality, there appears a precious lotus and on it a moon disc. In the center of the moon a beam of light, a syllable *Hrih*, appears. Concentrate on that, without duality, your consciousness sinking into it. From the beam of light, infinite rays of light radiate out to all of universal space, magnetically touching all the energy of the universe, all the four elements, transforming everything into radiant light. Experience total unity, a feeling of integrated energy. Your consciousness embraces the entire universe.

Now you hear the sound of *Om mani padme hum* resonating in space; it energizes the radiant light to reabsorb into the beam of light on the moon disc.

6 You, the beam of light, now transform into the mahamudra body of Avalokiteshvara: white, radiant light body, rainbow body, clarity body, profound body, crystal body, which can be seen through, in and out. So handsome, this divine body! One face, which stimulates such bliss just by looking at it. Four arms: two together at the heart signifying total unity and the other two held aloft, one holding a crystal rosary and the other a precious lotus.

Contemplate your divine Avalokiteshvara body, which is blissful in nature, without intellect, with the feeling of unity: "This is who I am." Let go. Just by seeing this most beautiful, divine body, bliss is automatically energized within you.

7 **Now your concentration moves from the divine body to the mantra at your heart, which radiates light into your Avalokiteshvara nervous system. The light then goes out, embracing and purifying all of universal space, the four elements, transforming everything into the mantra and all sentient beings into Avalokiteshvara. Everything is in the nature of transcendent wisdom and compassion. Continue to concentrate on the mantra while reciting it.**
Om mani padme hum, Om mani padme hum, Om mani padme hum...

8 Now you, Avalokiteshvara, melt from the feet upward and the crown downward into the moon disc at your heart; the rainbow light disappears. The moon absorbs into the mantra, *Om mani padme hum*, and this absorbs into the beam of light, the *Hrih*. The *Hrih* absorbs upward and disappears into empty space.

Again, in space appears a moon disc and on it a beam of light, which transforms into Avalokiteshvara's divine body. Concentrate on yourself in this aspect.

MEDITATION 7
MENTAL RECITATION AND HOLDING THE BREATH

Here is another technique you can use. First, meditate on the other stages.

7 Then, when you feel that your concentration on the divine body of Avalokiteshvara is good, shift it to the mantra. However, we will recite it mentally
this time, not verbally.
   At the same time use your physical energy, your breathing. While concentrating on the mantra in your mind, bring in your breath, slowly, gently,
and completely. Hold it. Then, when you need to, slowly exhale. Don't pay any
attention to your breathing; just focus on the mantra. This process makes it
easier to develop strong concentration, the realization of samadhi.
   When your concentration is good, you will feel that your breath has disappeared into your heart chakra. You will no longer feel its movement, as if
your breathing has stopped.

When your air energy moves, your mind automatically moves as well; they
move together. When you can control your breath, your mind can remain
still. Instead of constantly moving and being distracted, your mind will be
more concentrated. Even in everyday experience you can see the relationship between air energy and mind: When we get very emotional, our breathing becomes very heavy; our in-breaths are very strong and the out-breaths
are not.

According to modern science, you can't stop breathing and still be alive,
but according to Lord Buddha's science, you can.

During some sessions, concentrate on the form of the mantra as you radiate light out to all universal space, transforming all living beings into Avalokiteshvara's form and the universe into the mantra in the nature of
transcendent, blissful, radiant light.

In other sessions, once you have gone through the entire process—the
absorption and so forth, which helps you to develop concentration—just
concentrate on the mantra in your mind, rather than reciting it verbally.
When your knowledge of this practice is merely intellectual, it can seem as if
it's too much; but when you actualize it, it's easy.

And don't forget that you can recite the mantra when you go to the supermarket. But don't recite it out loud; whisper it.

13 ~ Closing the Door to Negativity

LOSING YOUR MADE-UP SELF

WHATEVER YOU THINK of as your "I"—"I am this, I am that"—your mind makes it up and gives it a name. When you check with intensive wisdom, nothing whatsoever can be found. It's just like an actor: One minute he pretends to be one person, then the next minute he changes his clothes and becomes somebody else.

Since the moment Tom got his name, every day, every month, every year, he has thought: "I am Tom." He thinks that Tom is something to be found within his body. His wrong conception believes that his self-entity exists within his five aggregates. Over and over again, he has continuously thought this. But it's impossible to find such a Tom; what he thinks he is has nothing whatsoever to do with reality.

The name Tom is given to a combination of shapes and colors, then the superstition arises. The idea was made up: "This is Tom," and then the wrong conception developed: "I am Tom." But actually, the moment the name was given, *that* Tom was already finished; the interdependent combination of various factors that was the basis of the name Tom had already disappeared. New aggregates, new colors, and new shapes arise, but constantly the idea "I am Tom" remains: "This is me; this is me; this is me." But it's just the mind making it up. Absolutely! Nothing can exist that is not made up by the mind; nothing has self-entity. The phenomenon of Tom is nonexistent. It is made up by the mind. This is reality. This *is* reality.

Whatever we are—student, farmer, anything—whatever name we give, it is always, "I am this; I am that." But it's completely made up by the mind. There is no self-existing entity there. All sentient beings are the same: "I am ant; I am cow; I am monkey."

We can all see scientifically that we are changing all the time, but we always point to our body and feel instinctively, "This is me." If you really look at this, you will understand intellectually how your conceptual thoughts make up such a self-entity.

The real experience of non-self-entity is when you come out of your samadhi and feel as if your made-up self has been lost. However, even without such a direct experience, you can understand reality simply through clean-clear, analytical wisdom.

Thus, you can understand that the divine pride of being the deity—"I am this; I am that"—is not totally made up; nor is it new. That reality is and has always been there; it's simply a matter of recognizing it. When the heavy, thick vibration of your usual projection of who you are has dissolved, you feel more sensitive; you have a subtler view. And when you have a more subtle view of phenomena, you have wisdom, you're more liberated; you have a view of totality. The fanatical view has vanished, the neurotic view has vanished, your miserable energy has vanished.

Such liberated wisdom energy transforms into the beam of light, and that in turn transforms into the rainbow body of the mahamudra deity—even more beautiful than a rainbow. Imagine that your body is that of a sixteen-year-old; just looking at this transcendent rainbow body stimulates bliss.

The divine pride of identifying yourself in this way automatically releases the hallucinated ordinary conception of who you think you are and of seeing yourself as having self-existence. Even though it is not actually nirvana, liberation, you can say that this blissful experience, especially when deep concentration develops, is like that—an eternal, blissful experience. And this mental energy is without limits, embracing all universal energy rather than being limited to this samsaric body and all samsaric objects. Whereas normal, superstitious experiences are shakable, this experience is unshakable. You reach beyond superstition. And you reach beyond mundane expectations, which bring conflict, indecision, and doubt.

Actually, you have the ability to stay in this experience forever, without coming down, but if you intellectualize too much about "How?" your experience is likely to disappear.

MEDITATION 8
FEELING OF FIRE AND SOUND OF MANTRA

1, 2, 3, 4, 5, 6 Guru Avalokiteshvara sits on a throne, a sun, and moon disc, in the aspect of a monk, with Avalokiteshvara at his heart. After reciting the prayers, Guru Avalokiteshvara absorbs into you, you dissolve into emptiness. Then visualize your mind appearing as the beam of light and, finally, manifesting as Avalokiteshvara. Contemplate each step.

7 Now, move your concentration from the rainbow body to the mantra at your heart, *Om mani padme hum*; this is subtler. The mantra surrounds the seed syllable *Hrih*, the beam of light. The *Hrih* and the mantra letters are white. As you recite the mantra, concentrate first on the seed syllable.

Then, when your concentration is strong, indestructible, imagine light radiating out from the mantra and the seed syllable at your Avalokiteshvara heart into universal space, purifying everything—all the sentient beings going here and there, all the things that grow, the very earth itself. Everything is transformed into blissful wisdom and all beings become Avalokiteshvara. Wherever you look, everything is in the nature of blissful light energy. Seeing everything in this way completely closes the door to negativity, jealousy, anger, attachment, and the rest. There is no way such emotions can arise; there is no space.

Now you, Avalokiteshvara, recite the mantra—first verbally, then with just your mind.

After that, contemplate the sound of the mantra without visualizing the letters.

Next, concentrate on the feeling of fire on the moon at your Avalokiteshvara heart.

Then, while continuing to concentrate on the feeling of fire, hear the sound of the transcendent mantra, *Om mani padme hum*. While you are contemplating the fire feeling, your liberated wisdom energy is simultaneously transformed into sound. The fire feeling is one with the sound of the mantra.

When you hear the mantra this time, instead of hearing the syllables one by one, you hear them together, all at once. This is a very important aspect of the technique. Feel it really opening your heart.

Concentrating simultaneously on the feeling of fire and the sound of the mantra has the magnetic power to bring all your wind energy into your central channel automatically.

Don't forget that you can help your concentration even more by adding the breath-holding technique I mentioned before (see page 113). Exhale slowly, gently, completely; then inhale slowly, gently, completely; then hold your breath and at the same time, concentrate. This is a shortcut to perfect concentration. Once you have developed it, you will experience both physical and mental bliss.

In particular, your blissful heart energy is completely linked with your entire physical nervous system. You feel almost intoxicated by blissful energy, which fills the nervous system of your Avalokiteshvara rainbow body. Experience a totally blissful feeling. When you develop this concentration successfully, you actually go beyond hunger and thirst. As well, you can produce blissful heat energy by actualizing this meditation technique.

MANTRA CAN HEAL

This kind of meditation can heal sickness—cancer, hepatitis, whatever. It's incredibly useful. Sickness is caused by unbalanced energy; the powerful white light can cure it. This is real healing. Mantra, in particular, is most powerful; just blowing on sick people after proper mantra recitation can heal them.

I had an experience of this at Sera College when I was about fifteen years old. I had a bad infection in my mouth from some growing teeth; my cheek was very swollen. I went to see my uncle, a lama, and while he recited a mantra, I would just sit there. This went on for a few days. Then, one day, after reciting the mantra, he blew on my cheek and *whoosh!*—all the pus came out. That is the power of mantra.

Reciting mantra around someone who is possessed by a spirit can cause the spirit to leave. And reciting mantra can subdue another person's anger; it can bring the anger energy right down.

Those who really practice a yoga method such as Avalokiteshvara are healers, because they are developing compassion. Sending radiant light out to all universal sentient beings is more realistic, more powerful, than simply saying, "I love you." Our usual love is mundane, emotional, small love: "Oh, yes! I will give you everything!" It doesn't have power. It's good, but it's not good enough.

If, through the practice of the yoga method, you experience the liberating energy of everlasting bliss and, with understanding, send out radiant white light, it is extremely powerful. You can't fight negativity if your energy is weak. An electric light illuminates a dark room much better than a little candle does. It's like that.

14 ~ The Two Obstacles to Samadhi

THE TWO MAIN OBSTACLES IN MEDITATION

THERE ARE COUNTLESS OBSTACLES that prevent us from obtaining perfect contemplation, but you can include them in two categories: one is called wandering, or distraction; the other, sluggishness.

When your mind wanders, it's often because of desire, jealousy, anger, and so forth. If it's desire for another person, you can contemplate impermanence and the nature of suffering.

Our mind wanders because of laziness. We don't make enough effort to concentrate because we don't yet have enough understanding of the result, or the goal, of concentration. We understand the result of going to the supermarket really well—all the supermarket goodness! We understand the results of our samsaric activities; but they are nothing.

The result, or goal, of concentration is eternal bliss, peace, an everlasting awakened state of mind. When you understand this, when you realize how worthwhile concentration is, will you not try to develop it? There is no way you can be lazy; you will have much energy and make great effort. You won't even worry about eating.

When you actualize the meditation we've been doing on the feeling of fire at the heart, you will get signs of success. For example, the bell will ring for dinner, and you'll think, "Oh, what a hassle!" I'm not saying that the result of concentration is that you don't experience hunger or thirst; but it's as if you're singing inside; it's such a blissful experience. You just naturally feel, "I could go without eating and drinking forever." That is the sign of success; it's not the final goal. It's like when you see the first light of the morning, you realize that the sun is about to rise. The light coming is a sign that the sun is coming up. Similarly, if you have the experience of blissful heat energy during your meditation, it's a sign of success, not the goal of meditation.

When you reach a certain stage of very deep concentration, the major obstacle is sluggishness, which has gross and subtle levels. Gross sluggishness is more easily recognizable; the subtle level is very difficult to see. You can easily mistake it for correct concentration, but it's not. You can stay there, without mindfulness, forever. That's dangerous. You could think that because the Western nervous system is so busy, this must be okay, but if it happens when you're in a three-year retreat, for example, you'll be in trouble.

Some meditators think they have perfect concentration; there is no wandering, no superstition, no sensory feelings, only a very blissful experience. They feel, "This is fantastic! Someone could cut me with a knife and I wouldn't feel pain. Now I no longer have any sensory attachment." The mind has indeed become more subtle, but it is not fully mindful; there is no intensive wisdom. It's like sleeping.

Maybe for most of us it will be a long time before we need to worry about this danger. But some people, because they have an aversion to the mundane world, they try too hard to attain samadhi. They reject everything and then have psychological problems. They go off to meditate and end up in a psychiatric hospital. It's possible.

In Tibet, we don't normally do this kind of intensive meditation in a group as we have been doing here. We receive instructions as a group, but we usually do retreat alone. The qualities of an ideal retreat place include peace and quiet, good water, and a beautiful environment. And instead of going shopping yourself, somebody cooks for you. You just meditate; then success comes easily.

Of course, for most of us, time is a problem. Nevertheless, we have had a short time here to gain some experience. We have had some satisfaction, but you should not believe that you can actualize in a short time the various meditations we have talked about here. It takes a long time. It's a gradual path. But these days, we don't have time so we have to rush.

MEDITATION 9
FEELING OF FIRE AND SOUND OF MANTRA 2

So now, let's do the practice together again. If I intellectualize too much, it won't come together for you. It's important to let go. This time we can practice the mantra without reciting it with our speech. We will do it consciously for a short time, and then we will shift to the feeling of fire. But first we will quickly go through the various stages of the meditation. By doing it over and over again like this, it will come more easily.

1, 2 Visualize Guru Avalokiteshvara, recite the prayers and offer a mandala. Now recite the mantra a few times.

Om mani padme hum, Om mani padme hum, Om mani padme hum…

3 Guru Avalokiteshvara's body melts into light, becomes an egg of radiant light. From the space in front of you it comes to your crown, enters through your crown chakra, and descends through your central channel to your heart chakra. It becomes one with your mind.

4 Now all the energy of your body also melts into radiant light and absorbs from the feet upward and the crown downward into your heart chakra…smaller…smaller…atoms…neutrons…totally disappearing into empty space. Your psyche lets go into empty space; no intellectualizing.

Experience nonduality without conceptualizing.

5 A moon disc appears in space, on the center of which is a beam of light. From this, light radiates out into all of universal space, even beyond this solar system, transforming all universal energy into light. All this transformed energy now sinks into the beam of light: this is your consciousness.

6 This transforms into Avalokiteshvara's rainbow body: white radiant light, like crystal, which can be seen through, in and out; a beautiful rainbow body, like a clear reflection in a mirror, in the nature of blissful, conscious, liberated wisdom. It is a clean-clear divine form, with no substantial energy. Just seeing such blissful energy stimulates a blissful experience in your mind. "This is who I am."

7 Bring your concentration into your Avalokiteshvara heart. On the moon disc is the feeling of fire energy. You concentrate on that, all the while recognizing that the fire feeling is a transformation of your blissful wisdom energy. Unified with that, you simultaneously hear the sound of the entire mantra, all at once instead of hearing it syllable by syllable as some kind of dualistic subject-object. Just let go; you don't have to work too hard at it. There's the fire feeling, into which your mind is transformed into mantra, and then you concentrate.

8 Now, your Avalokiteshvara body absorbs into the moon disc at your heart chakra; the moon sinks into the fire; the fire sinks into sound. Then the sound disappears into empty, universal space. Your mind goes into nothingness, emptiness, formlessness; no sound, no color.

When you have actualized the fire feeling meditation, you have reached the state beyond the recitation of mantra. At that time, you no longer have to count mantra; you have gone beyond that.

When you wake up from your concentration, you should hear all sounds as the transcendental mantra, see all forms and colors as the rainbow body of Avalokiteshvara, understand that all minds are in the nature of blissful wisdom, and recognize everything in the sensory world as hallucinations created by a magician.

15 ~ *Delusions Can Show Us Reality*

DEALING WITH DISTRACTIONS

WHEN DISTRACTIONS, mundane thoughts, come into our contemplation, we should not get angry or try to reject them. When superstition
arises, we should take advantage of it. "You're welcome! Would you like to
come in?" Mundane thoughts are your teacher; they give you realizations,
show you reality. Let's say the thought of chocolate cake comes into your
mind—it is easy to use distractions like this on the path to enlightenment.

First of all, why does this thought of chocolate cake come? Because your
previous experience of enjoying chocolate cake has left an imprint in your
consciousness. The experience itself has disappeared completely, but the
imprint remains, as if you'd sealed it, stamped it, in your mind. As long as
that stamp is there, the indestructible identification will also be there.

It's the same whenever you psychologically experience anything—happiness, misery, anger, bliss—it is never lost. It is imprinted on your mind, pro-
grammed into your mental computer. It is always there. This is memory.
There is a continuity between the past experience and the present recollection
of it. It's like electricity: the source is somewhere else, but the energy comes
through the various wires to where we are now, without a break.

So, although the experience of desire has passed, who is acting now? The
Tom who experienced desire in the past is completely nonexistent; the present Tom is completely nonexistent; but there is the recollection of the experience. The previous experience, the thought, the person, the object—
everything is gone, but still the memory of craving-desire comes, superstition comes, because it is imprinted on the mind.

When you understand that the experience of the chocolate cake arises
interdependently, you can see that it has no self-entity, that it doesn't come
from the object; it comes instead from your mental energy. You don't need
too much explanation to see this—it's simple, isn't it? The imprint of the previous experience of chocolate cake is always there, whether you are awake,
asleep, or meditating. Of course, there are cooperative causes, too: the feeling

of hunger, the arising of desire, and the object, the chocolate cake. All these come together.

We have to realize that the desirable chocolate cake is a complete hallucination. Objectively, it's not there; it's as if the imprint in your mind manifests into chocolate cake. You can check up scientifically. Where is that chocolate cake? It is a projection of your superstitious mind. Without the previous experience of chocolate cake, the thought of chocolate cake could not arise now. Your experience has nothing to do with *external* chocolate cake; your chocolate cake is an internal object. Your object of craving-desire is a fantasy, a hallucination.

It happens like this: Every time you recall the chocolate cake and craving arises, you're simply adding more petrol to the fire of your craving. And you keep believing in it as real. Most of the time we see things as real and believe them to be real, when in fact, they are like dreams.

So, whenever the thought of chocolate cake arises in your meditation, recognize with intensive wisdom that it is a hallucination, a mental picture, and that nothing exists out there. This will leave a strong impression on your mind. Then, whatever situation arises in your life, you will see it like that.

Remember, we discussed seeing a rope as a snake? Believing it's a snake brings fear, doesn't it? If you didn't have this belief, there would be no fear. It's just the same here. When you believe in the self-existent chocolate cake, superstition arises. But if, when seeing the chocolate cake, you recognize it as nondual, non-self-existent, this will bring some kind of dharmakaya experience. This is liberated wisdom because it doesn't bring the reaction of craving.

I repeat: When the mundane thought of chocolate cake arises in your meditation session, if you use intensive wisdom to analyze the object, you will see that it is just a manifestation of mental energy. It is only mind; no object exists. Because of your previous experiences of chocolate cake, you have the recollection of it now. The past has gone, the future has not yet arrived, so it must be a complete hallucination.

The key is skillful, indestructible wisdom. Instead of being caught up in hallucinated objects, you will have blissful experiences instead. Seeing chocolate cake as a hallucination automatically shakes desire, dissolving it, whereas believing in real, concrete chocolate cake increases the vibration of fantasy and, by reacting again and again and again, you accumulate deluded karma.

YOUR DELUSIONS ARE YOUR TEACHER

In this way you can use the arising of superstition as your teacher. In Buddhist terms, a teacher is someone who shows you reality. If we have both wisdom and method, all our experiences become our teacher; they show us reality. Learning does not come only from books. The wind, the water, the growing flowers—the growing beard!—everything can be our teacher; everything can talk to us. Our limited minds think knowledge is in the library. But for the person who really understands the graduated path to enlightenment, even the energy of a supermarket can be a teacher. Wherever you go, everything you see shows you reality.

You can see: During our meditation, and during our daily life, too, instead of being obstacles to liberation, distractions and superstitions can be helpful. They can help us realize the dharmakaya, emptiness. Our superstitions are kind: they show us the reality of emptiness. If there were no misconceptions, how could there be right conceptions?

By using our introspective wisdom, we can see that these hallucinations come from the mind. Mental energy is transformed into chocolate cake; it has nothing whatsoever to do with external chocolate cake; no such entity exists. Seeing this, we can automatically experience emptiness.

But don't rush; you can't rush mental energy. It takes time. Be patient; accept. It's not good to push yourself. In the beginning, perhaps, having the distraction of chocolate cake will get you down, but gradually, you will be able to put your mind back onto the object of contemplation.

Of course, it is better to have the thought of blissful samadhi rather than the thought of chocolate cake! As we talked yesterday: If we were to realize the transcendental experiences of bliss that we could experience from samadhi, we would definitely wake up from sluggishness in our meditation. It would give us much energy.

With intensive knowledge-wisdom, our penetrative introspection can become right view. After the superstition is gone, there is an experience of unity, of nonduality, and your mind can let go; you want to let go. Then, without pushing, automatically, you can easily return to the object of your contemplation.

Afterward, when you wake up out of meditation and resume your everyday life, before you do an action, you will be able to recognize the hallucinated, concrete picture and thus deal with things more easily.

MEDITATION 10
THE MANTRA WITHIN LIGHT

Now I want to introduce a new subject. This meditation is more subtle, more difficult. Yet, you can also say it's easy. You are Avalokiteshvara. At your heart is a moon disc. You visualize there another Avalokiteshvara—in the same aspect, with one face, four arms, holding a rosary, and so forth—but very subtle, very small, the size of a sesame seed. See it as very bright, clear, like a candle flame.

Does this sound complicated? As I explain it again, you can contemplate it. Each time you do the meditation, it gets easier; that's natural. Actually, the mind is so powerful, so beautiful. But sometimes we don't recognize the progress we have made in our meditation. We could have perfect concentration, but then we start to intellectualize: "How is my mind going?" We don't notice the progress we have made.

First, we can go through the various stages of the meditation.

1. Guru Avalokiteshvara appears in front of you in the aspect of a monk, wearing saffron-colored robes and sitting on a precious throne. His face is white and has a red vibration. He is looking at you with his peaceful, loving eyes.

His right hand at his heart in the gesture of giving Dharma holds a white lotus. Resting on its petals is a prajñaparamita text containing Lord Buddha's teachings on the perfection of wisdom, and standing upright on it is a sword, which symbolizes the knowledge-wisdom of all the buddhas. Fire radiates from the tip of the sword, burning up all your negative energy.

Guru Avalokiteshvara's left hand is in his lap, palm upward in the samadhi mudra, holding an upright Dharma wheel. He sits in the vajra position, surrounded by rainbow light.

At his heart is the wisdom-being, Avalokiteshvara himself, sitting on a white lotus and a moon cushion. He is white, has one face and four arms. Two hands are together at his heart, signifying total unity, and the other two are held aloft, the left holding a crystal rosary and the right a lotus. An antelope skin is draped over his left shoulder, which symbolizes bodhichitta. At Avalokiteshvara's heart is a white syllable *Hrih,* the concentration-being.

Also at the heart of Guru Avalokiteshvara is a blue syllable *Hum.* At his throat is a red *Ah,* and at his crown, a white *Om.* From the *Hum,* much light radiates out into space to all the ten directions, invoking all the supreme beings to come to him and sink into his heart. Guru Avalokiteshvara is now totally one with all the collected energy of all the supreme beings.

2 Recite the Seven-limb Prayer, make a mandala offering, and recite the Prayer of the Graduated Path.

3 The radiant light throne absorbs into the lotus, the lotus into the sun and moon seats, and they absorb into the body of Guru Avalokiteshvara. Simultaneously from his crown downward and his feet upward, Guru Avalokiteshvara absorbs into the wisdom-being at his heart chakra, which, in turn, dissolves into radiant light.

This light, the supreme nature of Guru Avalokiteshvara, comes through your crown into your central channel to your heart. Feel complete unity, total oneness.

4 Now, your entire being and everything else magnetically dissolves into light, integrating into your heart chakra in the center of your chest. Everything gradually becomes smaller and smaller...atoms...neutrons...and eventually disappears into empty space. Experience nonduality, contemplating everything with the right view of emptiness.

5 Your consciousness manifests as a moon disc. Upon it stands a radiant seed syllable *Hrih*, a beam of light, filling all of space with light. With part of your mind, concentrate mindfully on this light.

6 This light, your consciousness, transforms into the divine body of Avalokiteshvara. You have one face, four arms, a white, blissful, rainbow body, which is the transformation of the liberated wisdom energy of your own mind. This body is crystal, clean-clear. Your rainbow body is the essence of total consciousness: the unity of blissful experience and nonduality, which is beyond conceptualization. Contemplate this.

7 Now we will add the more subtle meditation. In the space of your Avalokiteshvara heart is a moon disc, and on the moon is another tiny manifestation of Avalokiteshvara, very subtle, the size of a drop of water or a sesame seed. At the heart of the Avalokiteshvara at your heart is an extremely bright light; radiant, like the flame of a candle. Listen for the divine sound of the mantra within that light: *Om mani padme hum*. This is possible. Your liberated wisdom contemplates the sound of the transcendental mantra within the light.

Even if you lose concentration, as long as you experience some non-duality, that's okay. Don't push; just let go. Or if you experience radiant light embracing the universe's energy, that's okay, too. Let go. Don't intellectualize. Be intensely mindful.

All energy has sound, as I have already mentioned. All four elements, or however you describe energy, have sound. We have this incredible machinery, this body, this nervous system; it's far more complicated than a computer. Imagine this nervous system at work; automatically, it makes sound. If you listen carefully, there is always sound in your brain; for me, there is always so much sound in there.

Sometimes from space you can hear incredibly beautiful music; it's natural. Really! I'm not hallucinating. Actually, there are lamas who have visions, and they hear tunes. It is a very esoteric sound. It's not like when an ordinary person makes up a tune. When these lamas meditate, they hear the sound of the tune, then they put words of prayers to the music. This is true. Don't think, "Hey, forget it! This lama is making magic!" This does happen. If you listen carefully, if you go to where such beautiful sounds come from, you can translate such sound rhythms into human sound. Yes, this seems strange—esoteric—but that's okay sometimes.

Remember, you can concentrate on the mantra. First you can recite it, counting each one. Then, you can practice reciting with your speech, but not counting. And then, you can recite it mentally. Finally, you can bring the breath inside and hold it there as a way of developing concentration.

PART FOUR

Mahamudra Is Always Here

16~ *Gaining Realizations*

THE REALIZATIONS THAT COME FROM
SINGLE-POINTED CONCENTRATION

THE RESULTS of successful contemplation are incredible, almost unimaginable. I will explain some of them.

First of all, you are able to effortlessly integrate the teachings with your mind. When you have achieved samadhi, you experience much bliss—not only mental bliss, but physical bliss as well. You experience blissful feelings in your entire nervous system. And whatever you contact with your senses causes bliss. For example, when you feel happy within yourself, even the clothes that you wear somehow cooperate with you, don't they? But when you are feeling miserable, the clothes on your body can irritate you. You're fed up with these beautiful things. We have this experience.

Normally, our body feels very heavy. But when you have developed concentration, it's almost as if you feel you have no body at all. The more concentration you have achieved, the more integrated you are, the more rapture, bliss, you will experience. The heavy energy of your body vanishes. You now feel so light, it's almost as if you can fly. It's possible.

You will feel very liberated instead of uncertain and full of doubts and conflicts. You'll always have a happy, joyful vibration. You won't notice the time. When we're miserable, the day is so long. Twelve whole hours pass so slowly. All day, the sun shining. It's so long until six o'clock; so long until dinner; and then so long from dinner until going to sleep. But when you're successful at contemplation, you'll hardly even notice whether it's night or day.

Actually, even now, when we have samsaric happiness, we have similar kinds of experiences. You dance and drink all night, intoxicated by the pleasure: the time just flies. "Oh, now it's morning already?" Well, this is what happens when we're intoxicated by the eternal blissful experience of mindfulness. We can see that time is not fixed by the outside; it's made up by the mind.

Also, darkness usually appears in your meditation. But when you've reached a certain level of meditation, you have an experience of light. Many people have this experience. Especially, you will have much clarity. You will feel that the nature of your mind is crystal clean-clear. Crystals reflect many things, don't they? It's the same with your mind. Our minds are so sensitive; they can experience many vibrations simultaneously.

And more. From successful contemplation you'll develop very fine sense perceptions; night or day, you'll be able to see all your environment very clearly. Your sensory experiences will be vivid rather than dull. You'll be able to see long distances, even other people's behavior, and their minds. At first, your experiences will seem a bit like a dream, but the more the concentration develops, the more clearly you will see, just as we are seeing each other now. Maybe you can even touch far distant forms. It's possible.

As a result of deep concentration it's possible to bring the deluded energy—the winds and the delusions themselves—into the central channel. This is similar to what happens at death, so sometimes in meditation when you experience this, you will feel as if you're disappearing; even the breath will stop. Beginning to experience the various visions associated with the absorption of the energy—mirage, smoke, and so forth—is a sign of good concentration.

If this happens, instead of being afraid, just let go; keep your awareness, your memory or mindfulness. At each of the stages of the absorption of the winds and the delusions, the mind gets finer, more subtle. But if you become unconscious, that is not right.

You may have an experience of space-like emptiness because to some extent the superstitions, the heavy wrong conceptions, will have stopped. These superstitions are like a huge cloud that obscures the sky. But if you are sensitive, when the cloud disappears, when even a tiny little bit of these elaborate hallucinations, the misconceptions, have stopped, you will automatically experience an empty feeling: space-like emptiness.

These are some of the experiences you will have when you have achieved single-pointed concentration. They are so worthwhile. They don't depend on your job, and you don't get them in the supermarket; you can never buy such experiences. They do not depend upon anything external, so they will always be with you.

It's important that you put energy into the practice from the very beginning. In the Vinaya there is an example: If you want to make fire by rubbing two sticks together, you have to persevere. You can't just give up and then start over; it will never work. It's the same with your concentration. You need to continue to meditate until you are satisfied with the result.

THE REALIZATIONS THAT COME FROM
DOING TANTRIC PRACTICE

Now I want to tell you about the realizations that you can experience by doing yoga methods such as this one and by reciting the mantra. There are many degrees of realization.

The highest, of course, is the achievement of the total unity of Avalokiteshvarahood; that is, by becoming a buddha.

At a mundane level, there are other experiences that can come. For example, once you've recited, say, ten million mantras, you will have achieved a certain level. If you need to have a long life in order to actualize liberation, you would be qualified to do a particular yoga practice to achieve this. Perhaps you could even be able to live for a couple of hundred years—don't be surprised by this, it's possible. Nagarjuna, for example, lived for five hundred years. And one of my gurus is about 120 years old at the moment. He is so healthy, teaching from morning till night. He is considered to be an emanation of White Tara, the buddha of long life. In fact, his parents and everyone in his village have long lives, too. There is a particular yoga method that you can practice in order to achieve this; we call it *tsering dzin*.

Another type of realization is the ability to learn the entire contents of a library telepathically, for example. You'd be able to read everything telepathically, nonstop, twenty-four hours a day. Perhaps you think this is too much, but it's true. There are also yoga methods that enable you to make yourself invisible. You could go to the bank and no one would see you!

Perhaps you think that this Avalokiteshvara yoga method is some small practice, but it's not; it's a universal method. Buddhism, in fact, is an incredible, universal subject. You couldn't learn everything there is to know in one life.

Another practice that you'll be qualified to do is called *chulen*, taking the essence. You can live on pills that include the essence of flowers and rocks, or even on the essence of stones, or on just water; you don't need any food. Meditators are living like this right now, in the Himalayas. For example, when the Chinese communists took over Tibet, many meditators just disappeared into the mountains and lived like wild animals. At first, your body becomes very thin, but eventually, you stay very healthy. Your body becomes so light, it's as if you could fly. And in meditation your concentration is perfect. After you eat a meal, if you try to meditate, your mind is very cloudy, isn't it? But when your stomach is empty, your mental energy is incredible.

Another practice is called *kang gyog: kang* means feet and *gyog* means quick.

You can walk incredibly fast, almost as if you were flying. Or you can learn to control people's minds with the use of mantra, actually getting them to do what you want against their will. In India and Nepal these days, for example, people use this power, but just for material purposes, which is not good and can be dangerous.

It is also possible to kill others, for a higher purpose, by using psychic power, mantra. Actually, there are many ways to kill, and in the Vinaya Lord Buddha explains the vow against killing in these various ways. You've all read Milarepa's biography, so you know about magic. Remember, his mother hated some members of her family who had harmed her, so she got Milarepa to use magic to kill them.

You can also control the weather, the elements. When we were in the refugee camp in West Bengal, there was always so much rain in the summer. The commissioner of our camp heard that we could do such things, so he asked us to stop the rain. I think he thought, "What do these people do? Just sit here and meditate? Now, at least they can do something!" We did the special meditation, and the rain stopped. And when they needed rain to come, they would ask us to help, and it would rain. He was very happy.

These capabilities are nothing unusual; they all exist in Tibet. For example, every village has a weatherman who can stop the rain. There is another technique: you put special blessed substances around your farm, for example, and the rain won't fall in exactly that area.

All this shows the power of the mind, the consciousness. Human potential is incredible.

17~ Your Wisdom Is Your Guru

WE HAVE SUCH FIXED IDEAS about ourselves: "I did this and that, therefore, I am guilty." These fantasies are released by the powerful, divine, radiating essence of the guru transformed into light coming into us. All our philosophizing and conceptualizing, the hallucinations of who we think we are, are instantly annihilated. When iron and fire mix, they become completely unified: iron becomes fire and fire becomes iron. You cannot separate them. It's the same when the powerful divine wisdom light comes: it burns all your projections of yourself.

You paint a picture of who you think you are, but it's a complete hallucination, having nothing whatsoever to do with reality. Your minds are so limited; you think "I am this or that," based only on your past experiences. You're not aware of the present at all, even when your eyes are wide open.

Also, we either overestimate or underestimate everything; we don't perceive reality. It's incredible. When we make things more important, more handsome, more beautiful than they really are, they appear more important or more beautiful, but it's just the projection of your hallucinating mind.

Let's say you're involved in some fantastic project and someone tells you that you are wrong. Because of your fixed view, you will freak out. But whatever you do, if you understand that everything is a hallucination—object, subject, environment, your future plans—you will be free. Someone can tell you that you are wrong, but because you are flexible and have no fixed view, you will accept. "Yes, I am wrong."

But this ego of ours always thinks, "I am right." You build up such a mandala, brick by superstitious brick, and finally, "This is my fantasy! It is perfect!" But you've built up something completely idealistic that has nothing whatsoever to do with reality. And when there are fixed ideas like this, there is fear, paranoia. You worry so much about what other people think. "Maybe he thinks it's nice; maybe she thinks it's not nice." Whenever there is superstition, it's always, "Maybe this, maybe that...." Even if somebody isn't thinking about you at all, you still worry about what he thinks.

Or, if you think something is fantastic but someone else thinks it's nothing: "He thinks I'm nobody!" You're hurt when they don't care. Ridiculous! If you *know* you are nobody, then you *are* nobody, so there's no need to worry! Enjoy what you are doing; accept what you are!

All this is because of our superstitions, our fixed ideas. We hallucinate this incredible dream world. I mean, it's more than a dream world! This is not something that you need to believe in; it's reality, isn't it? This is how we are. You can explain this to anyone, believer or nonbeliever.

Once you recognize this polluted way of seeing things, you can liberate yourself. Then you will have no fear about what people think of you. Lord Buddha's psychology is the most profound treatment. When you become yourself, you become familiar with your entire energy. Whatever you think you are melts into light when it's touched by the powerful supreme energy of the guru absorbing into you; you experience total unity.

In your meditation, stay with the experience of unity as long as you like; it's an incredibly powerful antidote to the fixed idea of who we think we are, of the wrong conceptions. Perhaps one day you stay in that experience, and the next day you become Avalokiteshvara!

Most of the time your problems come because you create fantasies. You think they are reality, and then, when things go wrong, you blame the situation. But you are not flexible. This practice, however, frees you: you can freely communicate, freely go, freely come, freely sleep, freely eat, freely drink. It is revolutionary, truly revolutionary. And it never harms; it is blissful in nature, so soft, peaceful, and liberating.

Sometimes you don't know who to believe. Someone says, "This is right," and another says, "No, that is right." Every time you practice guru yoga, however, you should think that your own wisdom is your guide. "Wisdom is my guru," you should explain to yourself. If we always rely on someone else when we have psychological problems, we will remain weak. "Guru" does not have to refer to something physical. There is the relative guru, and there is the absolute guru. The relative guru refers to the outside person, but the actual guru is your own wisdom. "The guru is Buddha, the guru is Dharma, the guru is Sangha," does not necessarily refer to the external.

It doesn't matter how much the guru talks; unless your wisdom is functioning, the teachings will go nowhere. But when your wisdom is functioning, you are liberated. "Who is your guru?" someone will ask. "My own small wisdom is my guru," you will say. "It guides me in a simple way." You take refuge in your baby guru. Every time you do guru yoga, you are taking refuge in the guru. My wisdom guides me, explaining to me my entire nature. That is my guru.

So, this practice of absorbing the guru into ourselves is incredible. Maybe it takes time for it to come together, but it is worthwhile. The powerful universal light embracing all the universal energy comes through your central channel. Because the energies of your body and mind are connected, everything will be purified and there will be an experience of totality: the darkness, bad memory, everything is purified. The light energy coming to your throat will purify impure speech and bring indestructible control, power. When it comes to your heart, you will experience unity of mind, totality, like the infinite blue sky.

The radiating light is supreme wisdom and, therefore, has the power to burn all impure energy. All your conceptions, your interpretations, are consumed by the wisdom fire. Psychologically, you will feel pure.

Slowly, slowly, practice becoming Avalokiteshvara. Remember, don't feel, "How do I become Avalokiteshvara? Does my nose become Avalokiteshvara? My ear?" I've explained this many times as it is such a difficult point for the Western mind. So check up, study. When you totally absorb the guru into yourself, you experience your own wisdom energy, your own totality.

18 ~ Making Every Moment Meditation

WE ARE SO FORTUNATE

D URING THIS RETREAT, we have all been very fortunate to be able to use
the freedom of our precious human rebirth in such a positive way; to
have taken this opportunity even just to get a glimpse of our everlasting peaceful energy, supreme energy, conscious energy, total energy. You have tried as
much as possible to actualize these practices. It has been most worthwhile.
When you put yourself in the right situation, the results will come.

While listening to the teachings on the lamrim, it can be difficult to see
how to integrate all the concepts; there are so many ways of expressing the various subjects. But when you act, when you meditate in a retreat like this, it
all becomes manageable. When you meditate, you can also see the totality of
your life. Normally, all you can see is what's in front of you; you can't see the
past and the future, the whole picture, what's really going on. You are too
obsessed, you have such a narrow view, and there is no time to see the totality. During such a meditation retreat as this, you can see the whole picture.
Actually, this is very good; you could say it's a realization.

Of course, lamrim meditations also involve contemplation. When you
have concentration, it's easy to integrate the teachings with your mind. Also,
when you have developed concentration, control is natural; you can put your
mind exactly where you like. Normally, we are the servant of our mind, which
is a mad elephant, running out of control at a hundred miles an hour. By having perfect concentration, you become the boss.

Actually, even just sitting here in this meditation position is training. It
takes so much energy; it's not easy, just sitting this way. Forget about actually meditating; you are learning to gain control just by sitting like this. Doing
nothing but sitting, just watching—this is fantastic. Just sitting in this position brings some kind of change within the environment of your nervous
system. It does, really. Incredible. In other words, sitting in this position itself
is knowledge. Okay. Maybe I'm exaggerating a little. But don't accept my
words; check up, experiment.

DURING EVERYDAY LIFE, DON'T BELIEVE IN WHAT YOU SEE

In Tibetan, we talk about *jeto chawo:* the action after samadhi. During retreat, this refers to the times between sessions, but it can also refer to our everyday life, when we're not meditating. When you have finished your session, which we call *nyamshag,* or contemplation, and have dissolved into emptiness—you, the mahamudra deity Avalokiteshvara, dissolve into the heart, into the moon, and into the beam of light, and then become smaller and smaller and eventually disappear into emptiness—you reappear out of this emptiness as Avalokiteshvara, and then, as Avalokiteshvara, go to work, eat your lunch, or do whatever you have to do.

It is important to practice like this. During your meditation session you feel good, transcendent, but after your session—or when you've left here and gone back home—you feel that you've gone from heaven to hell. That's wrong. In Tibetan, we describe this as *kangje lhagsub,* which means leaving footprints, trying to cover them up using your hands, but leaving more as you go. In other words, it's an endless task. Instead, you should take your good experiences with you.

It's important to have balance and continuity and not to feel that when you leave here, you've entered another world. If you feel like this, your practice is wrong; it's not integrated.

When you have finished your retreat, you should maintain the clarity of yourself as Avalokiteshvara, the mahamudra deity, and see all forms and colors as Avalokiteshvara, all sounds as the transcendent mantra, and all superstitious thoughts as transcendent consciousness. If you can't do this, then at least see everything as an illusion: see the various objects that appear to you as bubbles, as empty: "What I am seeing is not real; not true."

Why do you need to think this? Since we were born up until now we have been cheated by our concrete conceptions, our belief that everything is real. We always say, "This is real." Why? "Because I feel it is so," "Because I see it like that." Our logic is always "I feel," "I see."

We need to realize that what appears to us is like a bubble, that it isn't real. We need to develop the intensive wisdom that sees through the bubble and not get caught up in it. As long as you have the hallucinating mind, you will see as real whatever sense objects you perceive. This is not some kind of religious trip. We're actually describing reality, scientific reality. It is not philosophy, not doctrine. It is an experience that is beyond doctrine, beyond ideas.

You can see from experience that as soon as you give a name to something and believe in it, it appears to you. The saying, "You hear what you want to hear," is a good example. If you don't want to hear something, even though someone says it a hundred times, you will not hear it. This shows the relative nature of our mind.

Cultivate the understanding that bad is not bad and good is not good. Recognize that you are hallucinating a bubble. Then you will experience neither fear nor excitement; you will have control. You will reach beyond the extreme view and have a greater sense of unity. You will experience mahamudra.

Your mind is powerful. If you can have this right view for just two or three minutes, you can stay there indefinitely. Of course, it's difficult to do this at the beginning—we're like the new driver who can't put everything together and, therefore, can't let the driving just happen. But when you find the skill to put things together, to have the right view, and then, when you have developed the habit, your progress on the path will go so fast you won't believe it. Such is the power of the mind.

Another way to practice in our everyday lives is to perceive the various sense objects that arise in the same way that a magician perceives the illusions he creates—as interdependent phenomena. When a magician creates an illusion, due to the arising of various phenomena—the onlookers' hallucinated mental condition, a piece of wood, the magician's spell—a horse appears. The horse does not exist in the wood, nor in the magician's mantra, nor does it come from the hallucinations of the people.

This is important to understand. The magician sees the horse but knows it is not real; he doesn't believe in the bubble of the horse. His mind doesn't move; he doesn't get caught up. We call this *nyitsog*, which means to experience the unity of emptiness and the relative bubble; to see them simultaneously. Therefore, don't be like the ordinary people who see the horse: "Oh, fantastic! A horse! Look!" They see it as totally real; they become completely caught up in the hallucinated vision. Instead, we should be like the magician, who sees the hallucination but doesn't believe in it. This will bring an entirely different feeling than the feeling that arises when you see everything as having a self-entity.

BUT DON'T REJECT REALITY

However, although the horse is not real, the magician doesn't reject it, does he? He enjoys it; he plays with the energy. People come to watch; he makes money from it; he has a good time. It's the same with us. We don't need to reject our muesli, our chocolate; we should simply see these things as a bubble.

When you are in samadhi, contemplating your mahamudra divine body, you don't have any mundane thoughts. There is no bubble vibration, is there? But when you come back down from your samadhi, your old, dangerous habits are still there, especially when you go back into your usual environment. At that time, you need the intensive wisdom that sees through the bubble reality of your chocolate.

At the moment we are ordinary people. We see desirable chocolate and believe it has its own self-entity. But when we develop an understanding of non-self-entity, we see the chocolate but at the same time see it as empty. Eventually, when we become buddha, we won't have any dualistic view at all; we'll have reached beyond the dualistic view.

It is very important, then, to see your break times, and your everyday life, as sessions as well. After our meditation session ends, our practice should be to see things as illusory, as not concrete.

If your mind is divided and you feel that when you're out of meditation, you are so deluded—"I'm guilty! I have so much desire!"—you will not be happy. You think that meditation is good, is nirvana, but going to the supermarket, drinking, and eating are samsara. This attitude doesn't help. You're rejecting life. It's not necessary to think like this.

If this is your attitude, then perhaps only one minute out of twenty-four hours will be meditation; the rest will be samsara. This will mean that samsara is completely powerful whereas meditation is only an atom.

All you people who go to work might think, "I don't really like my job; I don't like my boss. I just go because I need the money." If you really understood that everything is a hallucination with no self-existent reality, your job, your experiences, would be fantastic. Every day, your activities would be the teachings, the lamrim. When you finished your job for the day, you would think, "Today, my graduated path to liberation session has finished. Now I'll go home." It's possible! I'm not joking.

We all have a life: a house, a wife, some children, a dog. And we have all these fixed ideas about what they are—but it's all hallucinated. We build up everything, piece by piece; it all becomes a total statement: "This is who I am." But it's all a complete hallucination and has nothing whatsoever to do with reality. If this were reality, then when you were happy, the picture of "This is who I am" would be real. But when you're miserable, that picture becomes "*This* is who I am."

If you really check up intelligently, you can see this is what we do. Buddhism emphasizes using our intelligence. We need to see how we hallucinate, how we don't see totality, how we're caught up in fanatical views and end up miserable.

It's not only in our mundane activities that we have these fixed ideas. If you were to come to a place like this with the attitude that it, too, is a mental projection, a hallucinated bubble, then you'd have no problems. Instead, you come with a concrete idea: "Oh, there's a lama teaching meditation at Chenrezig Institute. He had better give me realizations, otherwise, I might as well go to the beach!" You have a fantasy about the place even before you come here—that's why all you get is trouble, and you miss out on the chocolate.

The lamrim is not just the texts we study. All your energy, everything, can be the lamrim. Then you become a professional, a *lamrimpa.*

MAHAMUDRA IS ALWAYS HERE

Enjoy your life! Tantric yoga has powerful methods; it doesn't matter whether you are meditating, not meditating, or even sleeping. There are methods for putting yourself onto the right path at all times. When you wake up in the morning and you experience the sense world again, try to understand how everything is a hallucination. Then, because you are seeing that everything has non-self-entity nature, you will not react to the various problems that come. During the day, continuously see yourself as Avalokiteshvara. When you eat your dinner, for example, imagine each mouthful as blissful, radiant light energy going into your heart.

The Paramitayana view greatly emphasizes understanding the problems of desire and renouncing this or that: "I can't have chocolate any more. I can't even have a drop of water." If, however, you have skillful method and wisdom, whatever you do, all your actions, even those you call mundane, can become the transcendent path to liberation.

Mahamudra, emptiness, is always here. It is unchanging, permanent. It is not something special in some special place. If you think that samsara is your ordinary life and emptiness is up there somewhere—no! You will never find reality if you think idealistically and look for it in books or lamas. You will never find reality that way.

Spirituality is always here, too. We say, "Oh, I am looking for spirituality. I need to find lamas, priests, texts, bibles"—but spirituality is always here. It is reality, and reality is not dependent upon whether you believe in it or not.

If you look into the mundane, hallucinated bubble of everyday life, you will see reality.

Of course, the ability to remain in your contemplative state and simultaneously to do activities is the most difficult thing; only a buddha is able to accomplish this. But try to experience this. Then your life will be worthwhile.

APPENDIX 1

The Inseparability of the Spiritual Master
and Avalokiteshvara:
A Source of All Powerful Attainments

By Tenzin Gyatso,
His Holiness the Fourteenth Dalai Lama

Translation and annotation by
Sharpa Tulku and Brian Beresford

This sadhana, entitled *The Inseparability of the Spiritual Master and Avalokiteshvara: A Source of all Powerful Attainments,* was composed when His Holiness was nineteen years of age and was first published in Tibet in the Wood Horse Year (1954). This translation was originally made at the wish of Mr. Ang Sim Chai of Malaysia. It is our sincere and deep hope that people, through this practice, will discover a universal means of creating happiness through generating compassion and love for all. May every creature share in its boundless effects.

Grateful acknowledgement is made to those who assisted in this work. The language of the initial rough translation was corrected and improved upon by India Stevens. Thanks also go to Alexander Berzin and Jonathan Landaw for their helpful suggestions.

Sharpa Tulku

INTRODUCTION

> *To my spiritual master Avalokiteshvara,*
> *The full-moon-like essence of the buddhas' vast compassion*
> *And the radiant white nectar of their all-inspiring strength,*
> *I pay my deep respect.*
> *I shall now disseminate to all other beings the standard practice*
>   *of this profound yoga.*

The root of every inspiration and powerful attainment *(siddhi)* lies solely with the spiritual master *(lama* or *guru)*. As such he has been praised in both sutras and tantras[1] more than once. He is of fundamental importance because the basis for achieving everlasting happiness is requesting him to teach the undistorted path. Thinking of him as being inseparable from the specific meditational deity with whom you feel a special affinity, you should visualize the two as one.

The vitality of the Mahayana tradition comes from compassion, love, and the altruistic aspiration to attain enlightenment *(bodhichitta)* in order to effectively help all creatures become free from their suffering. Moreover, the importance of compassion is emphasized throughout all stages of development. Therefore, if you wish to combine Avalokiteshvara, the meditational deity of compassion, with your own root guru, first gather fine offerings in a suitable place. Sitting on a comfortable seat in an especially virtuous state of mind, take refuge, generate an enlightened motive of the awakening mind, and meditate on the four immeasurable thoughts.

PRELIMINARIES

I. Refuge

Namo Gurubhyah	In the spiritual masters, I take refuge;
Namo Buddhaya	In the Awakened One, I take refuge;
Namo Dharmaya	In his Truth, I take refuge;
Namo Sanghaya	In the Spiritual Community, I take refuge.

II. Generating Bodhichitta

In the Supreme Awakened One, his Truth, and the Spiritual
    Community,
I seek refuge until becoming enlightened.
By the merit from practicing giving and other perfections,
May I accomplish full awakening for the benefit of all.

III. The Four Immeasurable Thoughts

May all sentient beings possess happiness and the cause of happiness.
May all sentient beings be parted from suffering and the cause of
    suffering.
May all sentient beings never be parted from the happiness that has
    no suffering.
May all sentient beings abide in equanimity without attachment or
    aversion for near or far.

Recite these prayers three times each.

The Actual Practice

I. Purification

May the surface of the earth in every direction
Be stainless and pure, without roughness or fault,
As smooth as the palm of a child's soft hand
And as naturally polished as lapis lazuli.[2]

May the material offerings of gods[3] and humans,
Both those set before me and those visualized
Like a cloud of the peerless offerings of Samantabhadra,[4]
Pervade and encompass the vastness of space.

*Om namo bhagavate vajra sara pramardane tathagataya / arhate samyak
sambuddhaya / tadyatha / om vajre vajre / maha vajre / maha teja vajre /
maha vidya vajre / maha bodhichitta vajre / maha bodhi mando pasam
kramana vajre / sarva karma avarana visho dhana vajre svaha.*

Recite this purification mantra three times.

By the force of the truth of the Three Jewels of refuge,
By the firm inspiration from all bodhisattvas and buddhas,
By the power of the buddhas who have fully completed their
    collections of both good merit and insight,
By the might of the void, inconceivable and pure,
May all of these offerings be hereby transformed into their actual
    nature of voidness.

In this way bless the surroundings and the articles of offering.

II. Visualization

In the space of the dharmakayas of great spontaneous bliss,

In the midst of billowing clouds of magnificent offerings,
Upon a sparkling, jeweled throne supported by eight snow lions,[6]
On a seat composed of a lotus in bloom, the sun and the moon,[7]
Sits supreme exalted Avalokiteshvara, great treasure of compassion,
Assuming the form of a monk wearing saffron-colored robes.

O my Vajradhara master, kind in all three ways,[8] holy Losang Tenzin
    Gyatso,
Endowed with a glowing fair complexion and a radiant smiling face,
Your right hand at your heart in a gesture expounding Dharma
Holds the stem of one white lotus that supports a book and sword;[9]
Your left hand resting in meditative pose holds a thousand-spoked
    wheel.[10]
You are clothed in the three saffron robes of a monk,[11]
And are crowned with the pointed, golden hat of a pandit.[12]
Your aggregates, sensory spheres, senses, and objects, as well as your
    limbs,
Are a mandala complete with the five buddhas and their consorts,[13]
Male and female bodhisattvas and the wrathful protectors.

Encircled by a halo of five brilliant colors,[14]
My master is seated in full vajra posture,

Sending forth a network of cloud-like self-emanations
To tame the minds of all sentient beings.

Within his heart sits Avalokiteshvara, a wisdom-being,[15]
With one face and four arms.
His upper two hands are placed together,
His lower two hands hold a crystal rosary and white lotus.[16]
He is adorned with jeweled ornaments and heavenly raiment.
Over his left shoulder an antelope skin is draped,[17]
And cross-legged he is seated on a silver moon and lotus.[18]
The white syllable *Hrih,* a concentration-being at his heart,
Emits brilliant colored light in all the ten directions.

On my master's brow is a white *Om,*
Within his throat, a red *Ah,*
At his heart, a blue *Hum*
From which many lights shine out in myriad directions,
Inviting the Three Jewels of Refuge to dissolve into him,
Transforming him into the collected essence of the objects of refuge.

In this manner visualize the spiritual master.

III. The Seven-Limb Prayer

Prostrating
Your liberating body is fully adorned with all the signs of a buddha;[19]
Your melodious speech, complete with all sixty rhythms, flows
    without hesitation;
Your vast, profound mind filled with wisdom and compassion is
    beyond all conception;
I prostrate to the wheel of these three secret adornments of your body,
    speech, and mind.

Offering
Material offerings of my own and those of others,
The actual objects and those that I visualize,
Body and wealth, and all virtues amassed throughout the three times,

I offer to you upon visualized oceans of clouds like Samantabhadra's
   offerings.

Confessing
My mind being oppressed by the stifling darkness of ignorance,
I have done many wrongs against reason and vows.
Whatever mistakes I have made in the past,
With a deep sense of regret I pledge never to repeat them
And without reservation I confess everything to you.

Rejoicing
From the depths of my heart,
I rejoice in the enlightening deeds of the sublime masters
And in the virtuous actions past, present, and future
Performed by myself and all others as well,
And by ordinary and exalted beings of the three sacred traditions.[20]

Requesting
I request you to awaken every living being
From the sleep of ordinary and instinctive defilements
With the divine music of the Dharma's pure truth,
Resounding with the melody of profoundness and peace
And in accordance with the dispositions of your various disciples.

Entreating
I entreat you to firmly establish your feet upon the indestructible vajra
   throne
In the indissoluble state of *E-vam*,[21]
Until every sentient being gains the calm breath of joy in the state of
   final realization,
Unfettered by the extremes of worldliness or tranquil liberation.

Dedicating
I dedicate fully my virtuous actions of all the three times,
So that I may receive continuous care from a master
And attain full enlightenment for the benefit of all
Through accomplishing my prayers, the supreme deed of
   Samantabhadra.

IV. The Mandala Offering

By the virtue of offering to you, assembly of buddhas visualized
    before me,
This mandala built on a base, resplendent with flowers, saffron water,
    and incense,
Adorned with Mount Meru and the four continents, as well as the
    sun and the moon,
May all sentient beings share in its boundless effects.

This offering I make of a precious jeweled mandala,
Together with other pure offerings and wealth
And the virtues we have collected throughout the three times
With our body, speech and mind.

O my masters, my yidams,[22] and the Three Precious Jewels,
I offer all to you with unwavering faith.
Accepting these out of your boundless compassion,
Send forth to me waves of your inspiring strength.
Om idam guru ratna mandalakam niryatayami

*Thus make the offering of the mandala together with the seven-limb
prayer.*

V. The Blessing by the Master

From the *Hrih* in the heart of Avalokiteshvara,
Seated in the heart of my venerable master,
Flow streams of nectar and rays of five colors
Penetrating the crown of my head,
Eliminating all obscurations and endowing me with both
Common and exclusive powerful attainments.

*Om ah guru vajradhara vagindra sumati shasana dhara samudra shri
bhadra sarva siddhi hum hum*

Recite the mantra of the spiritual master as many times as possible.

VI. *The Prayer of the Graduated Path*

Bestow on me your blessings to be devoted to my master
With the purest thoughts and actions, gaining confidence that you,
O compassionate holy master, are the basis of temporary and
    everlasting bliss,
For you elucidate the true path free from all deception
And embody the totality of refuges past number.

Bestow on me your blessings to live a life of Dharma
Undistracted by the illusory preoccupations of this life,
For well I know that these leisures and endowments
Can never be surpassed by countless treasures of vast wealth,
And that this precious form once attained cannot endure,
For at any moment of time it may easily be destroyed.

Bestow on me your blessings to cease actions of nonvirtue
And accomplish wholesome deeds, by being always mindful
Of the causes and effects from kind and harmful acts,
While revering the Three Precious Jewels as the ultimate source of
    refuge
And most trustworthy protection from the unendurable fears of
    unfortunate rebirth states.

Bestow on me your blessings to practice the three higher trainings,[23]
Motivated by firm renunciation gained from the clear comprehension
That even the prosperity of the lord of the devas[24]
Is merely a deception, like a siren's alluring spell.

Bestow on me your blessings to master the oceans of practice,
Cultivating immediately the supreme enlightened motivation,
By reflecting on the predicament of all mother sentient beings,
Who have nourished me with kindness from beginningless time
And now are tortured while ensnared within one extreme or other,
Either on the wheel of suffering or in tranquil liberation.

Bestow on me your blessings to generate the yoga
Combining mental quiescence with penetrative insight,

In which the hundred-thousand-fold splendor of voidness, forever
  free from both extremes,[25]
Reflects without obstruction in the clear mirror of the immutable
  meditation.

Bestow on me your blessings to observe in strict accordance
All the vows and words of honor that form the root of powerful
  attainments,
Having entered through the gate of the extremely profound tantra
By the kindness of my all-proficient master.

Bestow on me your blessings to attain within this lifetime
The blissful mahamudra of the union of body and wisdom,[26]
Through severing completely my all-creating karmic energy
With wisdom's sharp sword of the nonduality of bliss and emptiness.[27]

*Having made requests in this way for the development in your
mindstream of the entire paths of sutra and tantra, and thus having done
a glance meditation on them, now recite the six-syllable mantra in
connection with the merging of the spiritual master into your heart.*

VII. The Merging of the Spiritual Master

My supreme master, requested in this way,
Now blissfully descends through the crown of my head
And dissolves in the indestructible point
At the center of my eight-petaled heart.[28]
Now my master re-emerges on a moon and lotus.
In his heart sits Avalokiteshvara, within whose heart is the letter *Hrih*
Encircled by a rosary of the six-syllable mantra, the source from which
  streams of nectar flow,
Eliminating all obstacles and every disease
And expanding my knowledge of the scriptural and insight teachings
  of the Buddha.
Thus, I receive the entire blessings of the victorious ones and their
  children,
And radiant lights again shine forth
To cleanse away defects from all beings and their environment.

In this way I attain the supreme yogic state,
Transforming every appearance, sound, and thought
Into the three secret ways of the exalted ones.[29]

After completing the above, recite the six-syllable mantra, Om mani
padme hum, *as many times as possible. Upon conclusion, recite once the
hundred-syllable mantra of Vajrasattva.*

*Om vajrasattva samayam anupalaya, vajrasattva tvenopatishta, dridho
me bhava, sutoshyo me bhava, suposhyo me bhava, anurakto me bhava,
sarvasiddhim me prayacha, sarvakarma sucha me chittam shriyam kuru
hum, ha ha ha ha hoh bhagavan sarva tathagata vajra ma me muncha,
vajra bhava mahasamayasattva ah hum phat*

VIII. Dedication

In the glorious hundred-thousand-fold radiance of the youthful moon
   of wholesome practice,
From the blue jasmine garden of Victorious Treasure Mind's method
   of truth[30]
May the seeds of explanation and accomplishment germinate and
   flower across this vast earth;
May the ensuing auspiciousness beautify everything until the limit of
   the universe.[31]

By flying high above the three realms[32]
The never-vanishing great jeweled banner of religious and secular
   rule,[33]
Laden with millions of virtues and perfect accomplishments:
May myriad wishes for benefit and bliss pour down.

Having banished afar the dark weight of this era's degeneration
Across the extent of the earth sapphire held by a celestial maiden,
May all living creatures overflow with spontaneous gaiety and joy
In the significant encompassing brilliance of happiness and bliss.

In short, O protector, by the power of your affectionate care,
May I never be parted from you throughout the rosaries of my lives.

May I proceed directly, with an ease beyond effort,
Unto the great city of unification, the all-powerful cosmic state itself.[34]

*Having offered prayers of dedication in this way, also recite others such as
the "Yearning Prayer of Samantabhadra's Activity" or "The Prayer of the
Virtuous Beginning, Middle, and End."*[35] *Upon conclusion recite the
following prayer.*

Conclusion

By the force of the immaculate compassion of the victorious ones and
   their sons,
May everything adverse be banished for eternity throughout the
   universe.
May all favorable omens become increasingly auspicious,
And may whatever is of virtue in the round of this existence or in
   tranquil liberation
Flourish and grow brighter like a new moon waxing full.

*This has been written at the repeated request of the assistant cabinet
minister, Mr. Shankawa Gyurme Sonam Tobgyal who, with sincere faith
and offerings, asked me to write a simple and complete sadhana of the
inseparability of Avalokiteshvara and myself. This devotion contains a
short glance meditation on the entire graduated path and the mantras of
the master and Avalokiteshvara. Although it is improper for me to write
such a devotion about myself, waves of inspiration of the buddhas can be
received from ordinary beings just as relics can come from a dog's tooth.*[36]
*Therefore, I have composed this with the hope of benefiting a few faithful
disciples.*

The Buddhist monk
Ngawang Losang Tenzin Gyatso
maintaining the title of Holder of the White Lotus (Avalokiteshvara)

NOTES

1. The sutras are teachings of Buddha dealing with general subjects while the tantras concern esoteric matters.

2. Lapis lazuli is a semiprecious gem, deep blue in color, and usually highly polished.

3. *Gods* are those beings who abide in the celestial realms, the rebirth state with the least suffering within the cycle of existence *(samsara)*.

4. Samantabhadra is one of the eight bodhisattvas of the Mahayana lineage. He is famed for the extensiveness of his offerings made to the buddhas of the ten directions. *Bodhisattva* literally means "courageously minded one striving for enlightenment." A bodhisattva courageously endures any hardship to overcome ignorance and the momentum of previous unskillful actions in order to attain full enlightenment for the benefit of all other beings.

5. The *dharmakaya* is the truth body of a fully enlightened being. It is the final accomplishment of all practices and results from an accumulation of meditational insight.

6. Four of the eight snow lions look upward, providing protection from interferences from above. Four gaze downward, protecting from interferences from below.

7. The lotus, rising through the mire of a swamp, symbolizes the purity of the bodhisattva who rises above the bonds of cyclic existence, uncontaminated by the confusion of the world. The moon symbolizes the conventional enlightened motivation of bodhichitta: the altruistic aspiration to attain buddhahood for the sake of others. The sun symbolizes the ultimate wisdom of bodhichitta: the direct cognition of voidness, the true mode of existence.

8. "Vajradhara master" is a name given to a tantric master, indicating that he is considered inseparable from Buddha Vajradhara (Tib. Dorje Chang, Holder of the Vajra), the tantric emanation of Buddha Shakyamuni. The vajra is a symbol of strength and unity. He is kind in three ways by giving the empowerment to practice the deity yoga of tantra, the oral transmission that remains unbroken from the Enlightened One himself, and the oral explanation of the tantric procedures based on his own experience.

9. The white lotus symbolizes the pure nature of the discriminating wisdom of penetrative insight into voidness. The knowledge of this is symbolized by the book of scripture resting on the lotus together with the flaming sword of total awareness that cuts through the root of ignorance. The scripture is one of the perfection of wisdom *(prajñaparamita)* sutras.

10. The thousand-spoked wheel signifies the turning of the wheel of truth *(dharmachakra)*, the teachings of the Buddha.

11. The three robes stand for the three higher trainings in ethics, meditative stabilization, and discriminating wisdom.

12. The golden hat of a pandit symbolizes pure morality. Its point stands for penetrative wisdom. A pandit is a master of the five major branches of knowledge: art, medicine, grammar, reasoning, and the inner, or Buddhist, sciences.

13. Meditation on the five buddhas, or conquerors *(jina)*, is visualized in tantric practice to purify the five aggregates *(skandha)* and to transform the five defilements of greed, hatred, self-importance, jealousy, and ignorance into the five wisdoms. The five aggregates are form, feeling, recognition, compositional factors, and consciousness. The five wisdoms are of voidness, equality, individuality, accomplishment, and the mirror-like wisdom.

14. The five colors are red, blue, yellow, green, and white. They are associated with the five conquerors.

15. A wisdom-being *(yeshe sempa)* is the actual implied being in one's visualization of a deity. Initially, in visualization, one conceptually creates a mentally manifested being *(damtsig sempa)* out of a relaxed but controlled imaginative concentration. This creation eventually merges with the wisdom-being when one's vision of the deity becomes nonconceptual.

16. The beads on the crystal rosary held by Avalokiteshvara symbolize sentient beings. The action of turning the beads indicates that he is drawing them out of their misery in cyclic existence and leading them into the state beyond sorrow *(nirvana)*. The white lotus symbolizes his pure state of mind.

17. The antelope is known to be very kind and considerate toward its offspring and is therefore a symbol for bodhichitta, the cultivation of a kind and compassionate attitude toward others.

18. The moon stands for the method by which one follows the spiritual path and engages in the conduct of the bodhisattvas. The lotus symbolizes the discriminating wisdom of insight into voidness.

19. There are thirty-two major and eighty minor signs that indicate the attainments of an enlightened being.

20. The three sacred traditions of Buddhism are the vehicles of the *shravakas, pratyekabuddhas,* and *bodhisattvas.*

21. *E-vam* is a Sanskrit seed syllable meaning "thus." It symbolizes the unity of the positive and negative aspects of cosmic energy which, in terms of the momentum from the past and the potentiality of the future, are unified in the present.

22. The *yidam* is the meditational deity with whom one identifies when practicing

tantric deity yoga. This should only be done after having received an empowerment from a fully qualified tantric master.

23. The three higher trainings are ethics *(shila),* meditative concentration *(samadhi),* and discriminating wisdom *(prajña).*

24. Even Indra, the lord of the devas, will one day expend the accumulation of virtuous actions that cause him to hold one of the highest positions within the six realms of cyclic existence, and he too will fall into a lower realm.

25. The two extremes are the beliefs in either true self-existence or nonexistence. The middle way *(madhyamaka)* shows a path that is neither of these.

26. The Great Seal *(mahamudra, chagya chenpo)* of the union of body and wisdom *(yuganaddha, zungjug)* is the unity of the clear light *(prabhasvara, osel)* and the illusory body *(mayakaya, gyulu),* The illusory body is the finest physical body, a combination of energy *(vayu, lung)* and consciousness *(chitta, sem).* The clear light is the wisdom of the nonduality of bliss and voidness.

27. The nonduality of bliss and voidness is the bliss of the direct understanding of voidness.

28. The heart wheel *(chakra)* of the central psychic channel *(nadi)* has eight divisions.

29. The three secret ways of the exalted ones are: (a) viewing all surroundings as a blissful abode *(mandala)* and all beings as manifestations of deities, (b) hearing all sound as mantra, and (c) intuitively knowing everything to be empty of true existence.

30. "Victorious Treasure Mind" is a name given to Mañjushri, the meditational deity embodying discriminating wisdom. His method of truth is the direct cognition of voidness.

31. The limit of the universe is when all beings attain full enlightenment.

32. The three realms are the desire, form, and formless realms.

33. Religious and secular rule refers to the form of government in Tibet prior to 1959.

34. The great city of unification, the all-powerful cosmic state, is buddhahood.

35. *Bhadracharyapranidhana (Zangpo chope monlam)* is the "Yearning Prayer of Samantabhadra's Activity." *Togtama* by Je Tsongkhapa is "The Prayer of the Virtuous Beginning, Middle, and End."

36. Once in Tibet a very devout woman asked her son, who journeyed on trading expeditions to India, to bring back for her a relic of Buddha. Although the son went three times, each time he forgot the promised relic. Not wanting to disappoint his mother again, he picked up a dog's tooth as he was nearing home on

his last journey and reverently presented that to her. She was overjoyed and placed the tooth upon the family altar. She then made many devotions to the "holy tooth" and, to the amazement of her son, from the tooth came several true relics.

Appendix 2 ~ The Meditations

THE TEN MEDITATIONS that Lama Yeshe guides the reader through are presented here altogether. There are eight steps, but each meditation does not necessarily cover all eight: one, for example, includes all except step 7, and another mentions only one step. Also, some meditations only briefly mention the steps. When doing the meditations, flesh out the appropriate steps, taking them from meditation 1, which explains the visualizations most extensively, or from variations that Lama gives in the later meditations. In all cases, for step 2 one needs to refer to the sadhana, appendix 1. All meditations should be preceded by the prayers of refuge, bodhichitta, etc., in the sadhana. The words in bold type show the new visualizations that Lama adds to each meditation as the course progresses.

MEDITATION 1 (CHAPTER 8)
BECOMING THE MAHAMUDRA DEITY

1 In the space in front of you there is a jeweled throne, held up by eight snow lions, which radiates light. On the throne, on a lotus and cushions of sun and moon, sits Avalokiteshvara in the aspect of a monk, wearing saffron-colored robes. Guru Avalokiteshvara's face is white and has a red vibration. His face is very loving, and his eyes are peaceful. His right hand is at his heart in the gesture of giving Dharma. It holds a white lotus, and resting on its petals is a prajñaparamita text containing Lord Buddha's teachings on the perfection of wisdom. Standing upright on the text is a sword, which symbolizes the knowledge-wisdom of all the past, present, and future buddhas. Fire radiates from the tip of the sword, burning up all our negative energy. Guru Avalokiteshvara's left hand is in his lap, palm upward in the samadhi mudra, the gesture of contemplation, holding an upright Dharma wheel. He sits in the vajra position, surrounded by rainbow light. He is simultaneously in samadhi and showing the aspect of teaching.

At his heart is the wisdom-being, Avalokiteshvara himself, sitting on a white lotus and a moon cushion. He is white, has one face and four arms. Two hands are together at his heart, signifying total unity, and the other two are held aloft, the left holding a crystal rosary and the right a lotus. An antelope skin is draped over his left shoulder, which symbolizes bodhichitta. At Avalokiteshvara's heart is a white syllable *Hrih,* the concentration-being.

Also at the heart of Guru Avalokiteshvara is a blue syllable *Hum.* At his throat is a red *Ah,* and at his crown, a white *Om.* From the *Hum,* much light radiates out into space to all the ten directions, invoking all the supreme beings to come to him and sink into his heart. Guru Avalokiteshvara is now totally one with all the collected energy of all the supreme beings.

2 Recite the Seven-limb Prayer, make a mandala offering, and recite the Prayer of the Graduated Path.

3 Now visualize that the radiant light throne absorbs into the lotus, the lotus into the sun and moon seats, and they absorb into the body of Guru Avalokitesh-vara. Simultaneously from his crown downward and his feet upward, Guru Avalokiteshvara absorbs into the wisdom-being at his heart chakra, which, in turn, dissolves into radiant light.

This light, the transcendent supreme nature of Guru Avalokiteshvara, comes through your crown into your central channel to your heart. Feel complete unity, total oneness.

4 Now, your entire being and everything else magnetically dissolves into light, integrating into your heart chakra in the center of your chest. Everything grad-ually becomes smaller and smaller…atoms…neutrons…and eventually disap-pears into empty space. Experience nonduality, non-self-entity. As much as possible, stay in that empty space, seeing, contemplating everything with the right view of emptiness.

5 After some time, if you are sensitive, you will feel, "Now a relative vision is com-ing." There will be signs of this. Before the sun rises, there are indications that it's coming, aren't there? Now, in that very space from which you had disap-peared, a moon disc, which symbolizes your consciousness, appears. Upon it stands a radiant seed syllable *Hrih,* a beam of light, filling all of space with light. With part of your mind, concentrate mindfully on this light, your own con-sciousness.

6 Now, from space, comes the sound *Om mani padme hum.* This acts as a cooperative cause for all the light to integrate back into the beam of light, the *Hrih,* which suddenly transforms into the divine white, radiant light body of Avalokiteshvara. You, Avalokiteshvara, have one face and four arms: two hands together at the heart signifying total unity and the other two held aloft, the left holding a crystal rosary and the right a precious lotus. You sit in the vajra position on sun and moon discs on a white lotus. Over your left shoulder an antelope skin is draped. Everything is made of radiant light.

As you experience a clean-clear vision of yourself as the deity, simultaneously experience divine pride: "This is who I am." This is the practice of the evolutionary stage.

This divine vision automatically releases your mundane view of yourself: your deluded, guilty sense of self. You reach beyond your ego's idea. It becomes a transcendent, blissful experience.

Don't intellectualize; just contemplate.

MEDITATION 2 (CHAPTER 9)
BECOMING THE MAHAMUDRA DEITY 2

1 In the space in front of you appears Guru Avalokiteshvara in the aspect of a monk, sitting on a throne held up by snow lions. His face is very loving, his eyes peaceful. In his right hand he holds a white lotus in which rests the prajñaparamita and, above that, a blazing sword. His left hand is in the meditation mudra in his lap and holds a Dharma wheel. At his brow is a white *Om,* his throat a red *Ah,* and his heart a blue *Hum.* Also at his heart is Avalokiteshvara, the wisdom-being.

2 Recite the Seven-limb Prayer, make a mandala offering, and recite the Prayer of the Graduated Path.

3 Now absorb Guru Avalokiteshvara into your heart. Visualize that the radiant light throne absorbs into the lotus, the lotus into the sun and moon seats, and they absorb into the body of Guru Avalokiteshvara. Simultaneously from his crown downward and his feet upward, Guru Avalokiteshvara absorbs into the wisdom-being at his heart chakra, which, in turn, dissolves into radiant light.

4 Then visualize that everything you are—your entire nervous system, your imagination, your body and mind—melts into light. This light then gets smaller and smaller until eventually it disappears. Now try to experience unity, the view of emptiness. Have a vision of empty space. This experience is not actual emptiness, but by losing your conception of self, your picture of who you are, you automatically feel a kind of emptiness. That is enough; just let go.

5 Eventually, out of the empty space, a moon disc, which is your consciousness, appears. Contemplate that. Then, at the center of the moon appears a beam of light, the *Hrih*. It radiates light throughout universal space, purifying all the impurities of all mother sentient beings and making offerings to all supreme beings. You don't need to think this; it happens automatically. Then the light absorbs back into the *Hrih*, which is you.

6 In space, you hear the sound of the mantra, *Om mani padme hum*. This energizes you—the beam of light—and you transform into the divine rainbow body of Avalokiteshvara. This is your own wisdom energy transforming into the mahamudra deity: white, four arms, sitting in the vajra posture on a white lotus. Your first two hands at your heart in the mudra of prayer, the second two held aloft holding crystal rosary and lotus. You see the crystal light body and simultaneously experience bliss and nonduality. That body is your mind. Your mind is object, your mind is subject: the unity of wisdom and method. You are the mahamudra deity.

Experience satisfaction. Don't think, "I want to see this, I want to see that; the face, the eyes…" Just see totality. Contemplate continually, your memory neither too tight nor too loose.

Your contemplating mind is not separate from memory; they are one. Your wisdom is memory. Intellectually, we think there is the contemplating mind and then there is memory, but they are one.

MEDITATION 3 (CHAPTER 10)
CLARITY AND DIVINE PRIDE

I In the space in front of you is Guru Avalokiteshvara. He sits on a throne held up by snow lions and looks at you lovingly. At his heart is the wisdom-being, Avalokiteshvara himself.

2 Recite the Seven-limb Prayer, make a mandala offering, and recite the Prayer of the Graduated Path.

3 Now visualize that the throne melts into light and absorbs into Guru Avaloki-teshvara's body. His radiant light body melts into the moon at his heart, simultaneously from the feet upward and the crown downward. Then the moon absorbs into the *Hrih* at its center, which becomes like an egg of radiant light. This radiant light enters your central channel and descends to your heart chakra, the essence of Avalokiteshvara becoming one with you. The egg-light radiates throughout your entire nervous system.

4 All the energy of your own body melts, dissolves, into radiant light. This light becomes smaller, smaller...atoms...neutrons...then disappears into empty space. Let go into nothingness, with one part of your mind understanding the right view of non-self-entity.

5 Now a precious lotus appears. On the lotus is a moon with a beam of light at its center. Concentrate on the beam of light. Feel unity with the beam of light; let your mind sink into it. Don't think, "Now I'm concentrating." Feel that your mind actually goes into that beam of light; don't feel that you are looking at it from the outside.

　　Light radiates out from the beam to embrace all universal phenomena.

6 Then you hear the divine sound of *Om mani padme hum* coming from space, energizing, stimulating the light to absorb back into the beam at your heart. Your liberated wisdom energy beam of light instantly transforms into Avalo-kiteshvara.

　　See each part of yourself clearly: your divine, radiant light body, as clean and clear as crystal; your two hands holding the rosary and lotus; the other two hands at your heart; your eyes; the antelope skin draped over your left shoulder. Everything is clean-clear. Concentrate on this clarity.

　　Do not feel that you are looking at an object outside yourself, as if it were another person. Feel: "This blissful, nonduality rainbow body is me; this is who I am." This is divine pride.

8 Now change your concentration. At the heart of you, Avalokiteshvara, there is a radiant light moon and upon it a beam of light. Instantly, your Avaloki-teshvara rainbow body dissolves into the moon, from the feet upward and the crown downward. The moon then dissolves into the beam of light. This becomes smaller, smaller...atoms...neutrons...and eventually disappears into empty space: experience nonduality, non-self-entity.

Now, in space, a beam of light appears on a moon, which transforms into Avalokiteshvara, which is yourself. See this clearly and at the same time experience the right view of emptiness. Experience this as if you were a magician who has conjured up, say, a horse: when ordinary people see it they think it is real, but the magician, who also sees it, knows that it is not.

In this way, experience the mahamudra deity.

MEDITATION 4 (CHAPTER II)
THE HALLUCINATED VISION DISSOLVES INTO LIGHT

1, 2, 3, 4 Guru Avalokiteshvara sits on a throne, a sun, and moon disc, in the aspect of a monk, with Avalokiteshvara at his heart. After reciting the prayers, Guru Avalokiteshvara absorbs into you, and you dissolve into emptiness. Contemplate each step.

5 When from space the moon disc and beam of light appear and the light goes out to embrace all universal energy, everything that the light embraces—all of Chenrezig Institute, all of Queensland, all of Australia, the whole world—dissolves, melts; all sentient beings, everything, melt into radiant light.

Make sure you transform everything into light, especially whatever you're caught up in, whatever attracts you. Psychologically, this is incredibly effective. The entire puzzle-conflict environment is digested, magnetically absorbed into the radiant light, so now you can't have any concrete vision of real beaches or oceans or mountains. That hallucinated painting dissolves. You no longer have superstitious thoughts about what's going to come from the kitchen: "I wonder what they're going to give me for dinner?"

6 Then, after this strong absorption with strong, concentrated awareness, the beam of light is transformed into the Avalokiteshvara deity body. In the whole of universal space there is only you, Avalokiteshvara. Contemplate the clarity of this.

When distraction comes, recognize that it is superstitious mental energy.

Instead of rejecting it, watch it, intensively, consciously—the bubble, the superstitious distraction, will disappear of its own accord.

MEDITATION 5 (CHAPTER 11)
RECITING THE MANTRA

1 Visualize Guru Avalokiteshvara in the aspect of a monk, sitting on a throne held up by snow lions. At his heart is Avalokiteshvara.

2 Recite the Seven-limb Prayer, make a mandala offering, and recite the Prayer of the Graduated Path.

3 Now absorb Guru Avalokiteshvara into your heart. Visualize that the radiant light throne absorbs into the lotus, the lotus into the sun and moon seats, and they absorb into the body of Guru Avalokiteshvara. Simultaneously from his crown downward and his feet upward, Guru Avalokiteshvara absorbs into the wisdom-being at his heart chakra, which, in turn, dissolves into radiant light.

4 Then visualize that you melt into light. The light then gets smaller and smaller until eventually disappears. Experience unity, the view of emptiness. Have a vision of empty space.

5 Eventually, out of the empty space, a moon disc, which is your consciousness, appears. Contemplate that. Then, at the center of the moon appears a beam of light, the *Hrih*. It radiates light throughout universal space, purifying all the impurities of all mother sentient beings and making offerings to all supreme beings.
  Then the light absorbs back into the *Hrih*, which is you.

6 In space, you hear the sound of the mantra, *Om mani padme hum*. This energizes you—the beam of light—and you transform into the divine rainbow body of Avalokiteshvara. This is your own wisdom energy transforming into the mahamudra deity: white, four arms, sitting in the vajra posture on a white lotus. Your first two hands at your heart in the mudra of prayer, the second two held aloft holding crystal rosary and lotus. You see the crystal light body and simultaneously experience bliss and nonduality. That body is your mind. Your mind is object, your mind is subject: the unity of wisdom and method. You are the mahamudra deity.

7 When you feel that you can concentrate on the divine body as long as you wish, you'll be encouraged to move on to a more subtle concentration. At your Avalokiteshvara heart is the six-syllable mantra *Om mani padme hum*. Concentrate on the mantra as you recite it. Recite the mantra loud enough for you to hear it but not so loud that others can. Also, remember that the mantra, too, is the transformation of blissful wisdom.

While reciting the mantra, imagine light radiating from it throughout all universal space, transforming the energy of the universe into light, which sinks back into the mantra at your heart.

Meditation 6 (chapter 12)
Transform everything into the mantra

I Visualize in front of you the inseparability of the guru and divine Avalokiteshvara, seated on a moon seat and lotus on a radiant throne. Don't think that you have put him there; instead, imagine that with his psychic ability he has come to you, in the space in front: "If you want me, look, here I am!"
Om mani padme hum, Om mani padme hum, Om mani padme hum…

2 Recite the Seven-limb Prayer, make a mandala offering, and recite the Prayer of the Graduated Path.

3 The radiant light throne absorbs into the lotus, the lotus into the moon seat, the moon seat into the body of Guru Avalokiteshvara. From his crown downward and his feet upward, he absorbs into his heart chakra, becoming a radiant egg of light. This egg-light, the transcendent supreme nature of Guru Avalokiteshvara, comes through your crown into your central channel to your heart. Feel unity, oneness, with Guru Avalokiteshvara.

4 From the egg-light much radiant light fills all your nervous system. Your radiant light body absorbs from the feet upward and the crown downward, becoming smaller, smaller, smaller…atoms…neutrons…and eventually disappearing into empty space, infinite in nature. Your consciousness goes into empty

space, seeing the nature of totality, no beginning...no end...no self-entity....
Let go of your mind into nonduality....

5 Suddenly, out of infinite space, nonduality, there appears a precious lotus and
on it a moon disc. In the center of the moon a beam of light, a syllable *Hrih*,
appears. Concentrate on that, without duality, your consciousness sinking into
it. From the beam of light, infinite rays of light radiate out to all of universal
space, magnetically touching all the energy of the universe, all the four elements, transforming everything into radiant light. Experience total unity, a feeling of integrated energy. Your consciousness embraces the entire universe.

Now you hear the sound of *Om mani padme hum* resonating in space; it
energizes the radiant light to reabsorb into the beam of light on the moon disc.

6 You, the beam of light, now transform into the mahamudra body of Avalokiteshvara: white, radiant light body, rainbow body, clarity body, profound body,
crystal body, which can be seen through, in and out. So handsome, this divine
body! One face, which stimulates such bliss just by looking at it. Four arms: two
together at the heart signifying total unity and the other two held aloft, one
holding a crystal rosary and the other a precious lotus.

Contemplate your divine Avalokiteshvara body, which is blissful in nature,
without intellect, with the feeling of unity: "This is who I am." Let go. Just by seeing this most beautiful, divine body, bliss is automatically energized within you.

7 **Now your concentration moves from the divine body to the mantra at your
heart, which radiates light into your Avalokiteshvara nervous system. The
light then goes out, embracing and purifying all of universal space, the four
elements, transforming everything into the mantra and all sentient beings
into Avalokiteshvara. Everything is in the nature of transcendent wisdom
and compassion. Continue to concentrate on the mantra while reciting it.**
Om mani padme hum, Om mani padme hum, Om mani padme hum...

8 Now you, Avalokiteshvara, melt from the feet upward and the crown downward into the moon disc at your heart; the rainbow light disappears. The moon
absorbs into the mantra, *Om mani padme hum,* and this absorbs into the beam
of light, the *Hrih. The Hrih* absorbs upward and disappears into empty space.

Again, in space appears a moon disc and on it a beam of light, which transforms into Avalokiteshvara's divine body. Concentrate on yourself in this aspect.

MEDITATION 7 (CHAPTER 12)
MENTAL RECITATION AND HOLDING THE BREATH

7 Then, when you feel that your concentration on the divine body of Avalokiteshvara is good, shift it to the mantra. However, we will recite it mentally
this time, not verbally.

At the same time use your physical energy, your breathing. While concentrating on the mantra in your mind, bring in your breath, slowly, gently,
and completely. Hold it. Then, when you need to, slowly exhale. Don't pay any
attention to your breathing; just focus on the mantra. This process makes it
easier to develop strong concentration, the realization of samadhi.

When your concentration is good, you will feel that your breath has disappeared into your heart chakra. You will no longer feel its movement, as if
your breathing has stopped.

MEDITATION 8 (CHAPTER 13)
FEELING OF FIRE AND SOUND OF MANTRA

1, 2, 3, 4, 5, 6 Guru Avalokiteshvara sits on a throne, a sun, and moon disc, in
the aspect of a monk, with Avalokiteshvara at his heart. After reciting the
prayers, Guru Avalokiteshvara absorbs into you, you dissolve into emptiness.
Then visualize your mind appearing as the beam of light and, finally, manifesting as Avalokiteshvara. Contemplate each step.

7 Now, move your concentration from the rainbow body to the mantra at your
heart, *Om mani padme hum;* this is subtler. The mantra surrounds the seed syllable *Hrih,* the beam of light. The *Hrih* and the mantra letters are white. As
you recite the mantra, concentrate first on the seed syllable.

Then, when your concentration is strong, indestructible, imagine light radiating out from the mantra and the seed syllable at your Avalokiteshvara heart
into universal space, purifying everything—all the sentient beings going here
and there, all the things that grow, the very earth itself. Everything is transformed into blissful wisdom and all beings become Avalokiteshvara. Wherever
you look, everything is in the nature of blissful light energy. Seeing everything
in this way completely closes the door to negativity, jealousy, anger, attachment, and the rest. There is no way such emotions can arise; there is no space.

Now you Avalokiteshvara recite the mantra—first verbally, then with just your mind.

After that, contemplate the sound of the mantra without visualizing the letters.

Next, concentrate on the feeling of fire on the moon at your Avaloki-teshvara heart.

Then, while continuing to concentrate on the feeling of fire, hear the sound of the transcendent mantra, *Om mani padme hum*. While you are contemplating the fire feeling, your liberated wisdom energy is simultane-ously transformed into sound. The fire feeling is one with the sound of the mantra.

When you hear the mantra this time, instead of hearing the syllables one by one, you hear them together, all at once. This is a very important aspect of the technique. Feel it really opening your heart.

Concentrating simultaneously on the feeling of fire and the sound of the mantra has the magnetic power to bring all your wind energy into your central channel automatically.

MEDITATION 9 (CHAPTER 14)
FEELING OF FIRE AND SOUND OF MANTRA 2

1, 2 Visualize Guru Avalokiteshvara, recite the prayers and offer a mandala. Now recite the mantra a few times.

Om mani padme hum, Om mani padme hum, Om mani padme hum...

3 Guru Avalokiteshvara's body melts into light, becomes an egg of radiant light. From the space in front of you it comes to your crown, enters through your crown chakra, and descends through your central channel to your heart chakra. It becomes one with your mind.

4 Now all the energy of your body also melts into radiant light and absorbs from the feet upward and the crown downward into your heart chakra...smaller...smaller...atoms...neutrons...totally disappearing into empty space. Your psyche lets go into empty space; no intellectualizing.

Experience nonduality without conceptualizing.

5 A moon disc appears in space, on the center of which is a beam of light. From this, light radiates out into all of universal space, even beyond this solar system, transforming all universal energy into light. All this transformed energy now sinks into the beam of light: this is your consciousness.

6 This transforms into Avalokiteshvara's rainbow body: white radiant light, like crystal, which can be seen through, in and out; a beautiful rainbow body, like a clear reflection in a mirror, in the nature of blissful, conscious, liberated wisdom. It is a clean-clear divine form, with no substantial energy. Just seeing such blissful energy stimulates a blissful experience in your mind. "This is who I am."

7 Bring your concentration into your Avalokiteshvara heart. On the moon disc is the feeling of fire energy. You concentrate on that, all the while recognizing that the fire feeling is a transformation of your blissful wisdom energy. Unified with that, you simultaneously hear the sound of the entire mantra, all at once instead of hearing it syllable by syllable as some kind of dualistic subject-object. Just let go; you don't have to work too hard at it. There's the fire feeling, into which your mind is transformed into mantra, and then you concentrate.

8 Now, your Avalokiteshvara body absorbs into the moon disc at your heart chakra; the moon sinks into the fire; the fire sinks into sound. Then the sound disappears into empty, universal space. Your mind goes into nothingness, emptiness, formlessness; no sound, no color.

When you have actualized the fire feeling meditation, you have reached the state beyond the recitation of mantra. At that time, you no longer have to count mantra; you have gone beyond that.

MEDITATION 10 (CHAPTER 15)
THE MANTRA WITHIN LIGHT

1 Guru Avalokiteshvara appears in front of you in the aspect of a monk, wearing saffron-colored robes and sitting on a precious throne. His face is white and has a red vibration. He is looking at you with his peaceful, loving eyes.

His right hand at his heart in the gesture of giving Dharma holds a white lotus. Resting on its petals is a prajñaparamita text containing Lord Buddha's teachings on the perfection of wisdom, and standing upright on it is a sword, which symbolizes the knowledge-wisdom of all the buddhas. Fire radiates from the tip of the sword, burning up all your negative energy.

Guru Avalokiteshvara's left hand is in his lap, palm upward in the samadhi mudra, holding an upright Dharma wheel. He sits in the vajra position, surrounded by rainbow light.

At his heart is the wisdom-being, Avalokiteshvara himself, sitting on a white lotus and a moon cushion. He is white, has one face and four arms. Two hands are together at his heart, signifying total unity, and the other two are held aloft, the left holding a crystal rosary and the right a lotus. An antelope skin is draped over his left shoulder, which symbolizes bodhichitta. At Avalokiteshvara's heart is a white syllable *Hrih,* the concentration-being.

Also at the heart of Guru Avalokiteshvara is a blue syllable *Hum.* At his throat is a red *Ah,* and at his crown, a white *Om.* From the *Hum,* much light radiates out into space to all the ten directions, invoking all the supreme beings to come to him and sink into his heart. Guru Avalokiteshvara is now totally one with all the collected energy of all the supreme beings.

2 Recite the Seven-limb Prayer, make a mandala offering, and recite the Prayer of the Graduated Path.

3 The radiant light throne absorbs into the lotus, the lotus into the sun and moon seats, and they absorb into the body of Guru Avalokiteshvara. Simultaneously from his crown downward and his feet upward, Guru Avalokiteshvara absorbs into the wisdom-being at his heart chakra, which, in turn, dissolves into radiant light.

This light, the supreme nature of Guru Avalokiteshvara, comes through your crown into your central channel to your heart. Feel complete unity, total oneness.

4 Now, your entire being and everything else magnetically dissolves into light, integrating into your heart chakra in the center of your chest. Everything gradually becomes smaller and smaller...atoms...neutrons...and eventually disappears into empty space. Experience nonduality, contemplating everything with the right view of emptiness.

5 Your consciousness manifests as a moon disc. Upon it stands a radiant seed syllable *Hrih,* a beam of light, filling all of space with light. With part of your mind, concentrate mindfully on this light.

6 This light, your consciousness, transforms into the divine body of Avalokitesh-vara. You have one face, four arms, a white, blissful, rainbow body, which is the transformation of the liberated wisdom energy of your own mind. This body is crystal, clean-clear. Your rainbow body is the essence of total consciousness: the unity of blissful experience and nonduality, which is beyond conceptual-ization. Contemplate this.

7 Now we will add the more subtle meditation. In the space of your Avaloki-teshvara heart is a moon disc, and on the moon is another tiny manifestation of Avalokiteshvara, very subtle, the size of a drop of water or a sesame seed. At the heart of the Avalokiteshvara at your heart is an extremely bright light; radiant, like the flame of a candle. Listen for the divine sound of the mantra within that light: *Om mani padme hum.* This is possible. Your liberated wis-dom contemplates the sound of the transcendental mantra within the light.

Even if you lose concentration, as long as you experience some non-duality, that's okay. Don't push; just let go. Or if you experience radiant light embracing the universe's energy, that's okay, too. Let go. Don't intellectual-ize. Be intensely mindful.

Glossary

*Note: Words within definitions that have their own entries
are rendered in bold.*
(Skt. = Sanskrit; Tib. = Tibetan)

absolute. The ultimate nature of reality; absolute nature; absolute reality;
   totality. *See* **emptiness**

absolute seal. *See* **mahamudra**

action tantra. In Sanskrit, *kriyatantra.* The first and most basic of the four
   classes of **tantra**, emphasizing external **yoga** and ritual purity. The practice
   described in this book belongs to action tantra.

Akshobhya. *See* **five conquerors**

altar. Representations, on a table or other surface, of the body, speech, and
   mind of the guru-buddha, and the offerings that a practitioner makes daily
   to them.

Amitabha. *See* **five conquerors**

Amoghasiddha. *See* **five conquerors**

amrita (Skt.). Nectar.

analytical meditation. *See* **meditation/contemplation**

Asanga. Indian Buddhist master of the fifth century C.E.; along with **Nagarjuna**, one of the Two Jewels of the Southern Continent revered for spreading **Mahayana** Buddhism; founder of the Yogachara school of Buddhist
   philosophy.

Atisha (982–1054). Indian Buddhist master who reintroduced Buddhism
   into Tibet after its suppression by the antireligious King Langdarma;
   author of the influential **lamrim** text *Lamp for the Path to Enlightenment.*

Avalokiteshvara. Chenrezig (Tib.). Literally, he who looks down upon the world with eyes of compassion. Meditational **deity** embodying the compassion of all enlightened beings.

Avalokiteshvarahood. *See* **enlightenment**

bodhichitta (Skt.). Literally, enlightenment mind. The effortless and continuously present altruistic wish in the minds of **bodhisattvas** to achieve **enlightenment** for the sake of all **sentient beings**.

bodhisattva (Skt.). Literally, enlightenment(-bound) being. One who possesses **bodhichitta.**

buddha (Skt.). A fully enlightened being, such as **Shakyamuni Buddha**, founder of Buddhism; first of the **Three Precious Jewels.**

Buddhadharma. *See* **Dharma**

buddhahood. *See* **enlightenment**

central channel. According to **tantra**, the subtle energy pathway running from the crown of one's head down to below the navel and along which the **chakras** are located.

calm abiding. *See* **single-pointed concentration**

chakra (Skt.). Literally, wheel. Any one of the several places along the **central channel** where restrictions in the flow of wind energy occur.

Chandrakirti. The sixth-century Indian pandit, a disciple of **Nagarjuna**, who elucidated Nagarjuna's exposition of the middle way (**madhyamaka**), presenting it specifically as what is now known as the view of the Prasangika-Madhyamaka (or Middle Way Consequentialist) school, whose texts are the basis of the study of the middle way in all Tibetan traditions.

Chenrezig (Tib.). *See* **Avalokiteshvara**

Chenrezig Institute. A Buddhist center in Queensland, Australia, part of the Foundation for the Preservation of the **Mahayana** Tradition, an organization established by Lama Yeshe. This teaching was given there in 1976.

clarity. Also known as clear appearance, the vivid appearance of oneself as a particular meditational **deity**, cultivated in tantric practice along with **divine pride.**

concentration-being. The subtle essence of the meditational **deity**, visualized as the Sanskrit syllable *Hrih* or a beam of light, from which one manifests as the meditational deity itself.

contemplation. *See* **meditation/contemplation**

Dalai Lama. *See* **His Holiness the Dalai Lama**

deity. A divine being; a **buddha**, such as **Avalokiteshvara**, with whom a meditator identifies during tantric practice. Also called a meditational deity, or *yidam* in Tibetan.

delusion. Hallucination; misconception; negative mind; negative energy; negativity; superstition; wrong conception. Any mental or emotional state that, when it arises, disturbs one's peace of mind and causes one to harm others and thus create negative **karma**. Chief among these negative states of mind are **ignorance**, attachment, anger, jealousy, and pride.

dependent arising. Relative; interdependent. The way that the self and all phenomena exist conventionally: they come into being in dependence upon causes and conditions, upon their parts, and, most subtly, upon the mind imputing, or labeling, them.

Dharma (Skt.). In general, spiritual practice; specifically, the Buddhist teachings; Buddhadharma; that which protects one from suffering and leads to **liberation** and **enlightenment**; second of the **Three Precious Jewels**.

dharmachakra (Skt.). Literally, wheel of Dharma. Eight-spoked wheel symbolic of Buddha's teachings, the turning of which symbolizes the spread of the Buddhadharma or the reintroduction of these teachings into the world after they have disappeared.

dharmakaya (Skt.). Literally, truth body. The omniscient and compassionate mind of a **buddha**. Often used here as a synonym for **emptiness**.

divine pride. The tantric practitioners' strong conviction of actually being the **deity** they are visualizing themselves as in their **meditation**; combined with the practice of **clarity**, or clear appearance.

dualistic view. *See* **ignorance**

empowerment. *See* **initiation**

emptiness. Nonduality; non-self-entity; non-self-existence; totality. The absolute nature of the self and all phenomena. Ultimately, everything lacks, or is empty of, existing dualistically, inherently, truly, from its own side.

enlightenment. Buddhahood; omniscience; totality; full enlightenment; awakening; tathagatahood; Avalokiteshvarahood; unification; union of method and wisdom. The ultimate goal of **Mahayana** Buddhist practice and the potential of all **sentient beings**, enlightenment is characterized by (1) infinite wisdom, which knows the reality of all phenomena and sees perfectly the minds of every **sentient being**; (2) infinite compassion, the spontaneous and continuous wish to free all sentient beings from suffering and lead them to enlightenment; and (3) infinite power, the capacity to do whatever needs to be done to achieve this.

evolutionary stage. Generation stage. A term borrowed from **highest yoga tantra**, also used here to refer to the practice of visualizing oneself as the meditational **deity**.

five aggregates. The mental and physical components of **sentient beings**: form, feeling, discrimination, compositional factors, and consciousness.

five conquerors. In Sanskrit, *jinas*. Often known as the five dhyani **buddhas**. The heads of the five buddha lineages, or families: Akshobhya, Vairochana, Ratnasambhava, Amitabha, and Amoghasiddha. They represent (1) the purification of one's contaminated aggregates—respectively, consciousness, form, feeling, discrimination, and compositional factors; (2) the **purification** of various **delusions**—respectively, **ignorance**, anger, pride, attachment, and jealousy; and (3) the attainment of exalted wisdoms—respectively, dharmadhatu, mirror-like, equality, discriminating, and all-accomplishing exalted wisdom.

four classes of tantra. The division of tantric practice into **action** *(kriya)*, performance, yoga, and **highest yoga tantra**.

four elements. Earth, water, fire, and air or wind, which, with the channels and the kundalini, constitute the six distinctive characteristics of the human body. See **central channel.**

four immeasurable thoughts. Four immeasurables: love, compassion, joy, and equanimity.

four noble truths. The subject of **Shakyamuni Buddha**'s first discourse in which he explained (1) that there is suffering; (2) that this suffering has identifiable causes; (3) that it is possible to cease this suffering; and (4) the methods for getting rid of suffering.

Gelug (Tib.). Literally, virtuous ones. One of the four traditions of Tibetan Buddhism, founded by **Lama Je Tsongkhapa** in the early fifteenth century and propagated by such illustrious masters as the successive **Dalai Lamas** and Panchen Lamas.

generation stage. *See* **evolutionary stage**

geshe (Tib). Literally, spiritual friend. Title accorded those who have successfully completed a rigorous course of study of at least twenty years at one of the major **Gelug** monasteries originally located in Tibet and now relocated in India.

Khensur Rinpoche Jampa Tegchog. Former abbot of Sera Je Monastery in India and **FPMT**'s Nalanda Monastery in France.

god. Occupant of the highest, most pleasurable realm within the desire realm of **samsara**.

graduated path. *See* **lamrim**

guru (Skt.). Spiritual master; virtuous friend. Literally, heavy, as in heavy with **Dharma** knowledge. One's spiritual guide, teacher, or master. In Tibetan, *lama;* literally, superior one.

Guru Avalokiteshvara. One's own spiritual master, or guru, seen as inseparably one with Buddha Avalokiteshvara. In this practice, the guru visualized is His Holiness the **Dalai Lama**.

guru mantra. A Sanskrit **mantra** incorporating the name of one's own **guru**.

guru devotion. The attitude of respect and faith developed by the practitioner toward their **guru**, the highest level of which, in **tantra**, is seeing the guru as without fault, as a **buddha**, formalized in the practice of **guru yoga**; the root of all realizations on the path to **enlightenment**.

guru yoga (Skt.). The tantric practice of **guru devotion** in which the practitioner visualizes being inseparably one with **Guru Avalokiteshvara**, for example.

hallucination. *See* **delusion**

hell being. Inhabitant of the lowest, most suffering realm within **samsara**, plagued by heat and cold and other extreme forms of torment. See **samsara**.

highest yoga tantra. In Sanskrit, *maha-anuttarayogatantra*. The fourth and supreme class of **tantra**, consisting of both **evolutionary** and completion stages, which must be accomplished in order to achieve **enlightenment**.

Hinayana (Skt.). Literally, the Lesser Vehicle. The Buddhist path to **nirvana**.

Hinduism. The main religion of India.

His Holiness the Dalai Lama. Temporal and spiritual leader of the Tibetan people, recognized as the human manifestation of **Avalokiteshvara**. The current Dalai Lama, the fourteenth in his lineage, was born in 1935 and heads the Tibetan government-in-exile in Dharamsala, India. Author of *The Inseparability of the Spiritual Master and Avalokiteshvara: A Source of All Powerful Attainments*, the basis of this commentary by Lama Yeshe.

hungry ghost. In Sanskrit, *preta*. Being inhabiting the second lowest realm within **samsara**, plagued by insatiable hunger and thirst.

ignorance. The mistaken way of seeing oneself and the world, causing one to grasp instinctively at all things as being **self-existent**, as having a self-entity. This root **delusion** is the source of the other delusions, such as attachment, anger, and jealousy.

initiation. Empowerment. The transmission from a tantric master to a disciple of the practice of a particular **deity**, which permits the disciple to engage in that practice.

interdependent. *See* **dependent arising**

karma (Skt.). Literally, action. The law of cause and effect: the process whereby positive actions of body, speech, and mind lead to happiness in future lives, and negative ones to suffering. Buddha's explanation of why beings experience happiness and suffering.

Kopan Monastery. Founded in the Kathmandu Valley of Nepal in 1969 by Lama Thubten Yeshe and Lama Thubten Zopa Rinpoche, where some three hundred monks study in the tradition of the monastic universities of Tibet and which runs courses year-round for Westerners and other foreigners.

kriya tantra. *See* **action tantra**

lama (Tib.). *See* **guru**

Lama Je Tsongkhapa (1357–1419). The **mahasiddha** scholar who founded the **Gelug** tradition of Tibetan Buddhism.

lamrim (Tib.). Literally, stages of the path, graduated path. Originally outlined in Tibet by Lama **Atisha** in the eleventh century in his *Lamp for the Path to Enlightenment,* the lamrim is a step-by-step arrangement of Buddha's teachings, presented as meditations to be actualized, incorporating **Hinayana**, **Paramitayana**, and **Tantrayana**.

liberation. *See* **nirvana**

Lord Buddha. *See* **Shakyamuni Buddha**

lower realms. *See* **samsara**

Madhyamaka (Skt.). Literally, middle way. The school of philosophy founded by **Nagarjuna.**

mahamudra (Skt.). Literally, great seal. Used here synonymously with the **emptiness** of all phenomena. In Tibetan Buddhism, there are methods called mahamudra that enable the practitioner to realize the emptiness of one's own mind in particular.

mahasiddha (Skt.). Literally, greatly accomplished one. A highly realized tantric practitioner.

Mahayana (Skt.). Literally, Great Vehicle. The path of the **bodhisattvas**, the ultimate goal of which is buddhahood; includes both **Paramitayana** and **Tantrayana.**

Maitreya. The fifth of the one thousand founding buddhas of this present world age, who is predicted to turn the wheel of **Dharma** after the teachings of **Shakyamuni Buddha** have disappeared. Teacher who revealed the true meaning of the *prajñaparamita* (perfection of wisdom) sutras to **Asanga.**

mandala (Skt.). The purified environment of a **deity**; the diagram or painting representing this.

mandala offerings. The visualized offering to the Guru Buddha, in this case **Guru Avalokiteshvara**, of the entire universe.

Manjushri (Skt.). A male **buddha** embodying the wisdom of **emptiness**.

mantra (Skt.). Literally, protection of the mind, in the sense of protecting one's mind from ordinary appearances and conceptions, from seeing oneself and other phenomena as mundane; Sanskrit syllables, recited in conjunction with the practice of a particular **deity**, that embody the qualities of that deity.

Mantrayana. *See* **Tantrayana**

meditation/contemplation. The process whereby a spiritual practitioner becomes increasingly familiar with a **Dharma** topic, leading to realization and self-transformation. There are two modes of meditation—concentration and insight. 1. *Insight:* within **sutra** practices, meditators utilize reasoning and logical analysis to investigate the meaning and validity of a particular teaching; and within tantric practice, they utilize visualization. 2. *Concentration:* then the practitioner focuses single-pointedly on the insight that arises from analysis or on the visualization, thus stabilizing and deepening the insight. When single-pointed concentration has been achieved, insights can be perfected.

meditational deity. *See* **deity**

method and wisdom. Referring respectively to the realizations of compassion and **emptiness**, method and wisdom include all the practices leading to full **enlightenment**.

Milarepa. Eleventh-century **yogi**, saint, and poet, a favorite of all Tibetans.

misconception. *See* **delusion**

Mount Meru. According to Indian cosmology, the center of the universe.

Nagarjuna. The Indian scholar and tantric adept, born approximately four hundred years after Buddha's passing away, who clarified Buddha's teachings on emptiness; founder of the **Madhyamaka** school of Buddhist philosophy; along with **Asanga**, one of the Two Jewels of the Southern Continent revered for spreading **Mahayana** Buddhism.

negative mind. *See* **delusion**

negativity. *See* **delusion**

nirvana (Skt.). Self-liberation; self-realization; tranquil liberation. Literally, cessation of suffering. Liberation from suffering, from having to be reborn in **samsara**, achieved when all **delusions** have been abandoned; the goal of the **Hinayana** practitioner.

nonduality. *See* **emptiness**

non-self-entity. *See* **emptiness**

non-self-existence. *See* **emptiness**

Pabongkha Rinpoche. Famous **Gelug** lama (1878–1941), the root **guru** of Lama Yeshe's main teachers.

Paramitayana (Skt.). Literally, Perfection Vehicle. The **bodhisattva** vehicle; the **Mahayana sutra** teachings; the part of the Mahayana that does not include **tantra**.

perfection. *See* **enlightenment**

Perfection Vehicle. *See* **Paramitayana**

prajñaparamita (Skt.). Literally, perfection of wisdom; one of the six **bodhisattva** perfections; a collection of **sutra** teachings by Lord Buddha on the wisdom of **emptiness**.

preta (Skt.). Hungry ghost. *See also* **samsara**

purification. The removal, or cleansing, from the mind of negative **karma** and its imprints. See discussion of the *four opponent powers* in the introduction.

Ratnasambhava. *See* **five conquerors**

realization. Experiential insight into the meaning of **emptiness, impermanence, karma,** etc., gained in meditation.

refuge. The heartfelt reliance upon **Buddha, Dharma**, and **Sangha** for guidance on the path to **enlightenment.**

renunciation. The fervent wish to be free of suffering based on the realization that samsaric enjoyments are incapable of providing lasting happiness and that **karma** and **delusions** are the cause of one's suffering.

right view. Insight into **emptiness.**

Rinpoche (Tib.). Literally, precious one. An honorific term given to recognized reincarnations of great practitioners; a respectful title used for one's own **guru** or other lamas.

sadhana (Skt.). Literally, method of accomplishment. The step-by-step set of **meditations** and prayers related to a particular **deity**.

samadhi (Skt.). The state of profound and subtle awareness achieved in single-pointed concentration **meditation**.

Samantabhadra. A **bodhisattva** noted for his offerings.

samsara (Skt.). Literally, wandering, circling; cyclic existence. The six realms of samsara include the three lower (i.e., more suffering) realms of the **hell beings**, **hungry ghosts**, and animals, and the three upper (i.e., comparatively less suffering) realms of the humans, demigods, and **gods**. **Samsara** is the continuous process of death and rebirth within these six realms, caused by **karma** and perpetuated by **delusions**.

Sangha (Skt.). Spiritual community; third of the **Three Precious Jewels**.

secret mantra. *See* **Tantrayana**

self-entity. *See* **self-existence**

self-existence. Truly existent self; inherently existent self; self-entity. The type of existence that the self and all phenomena appear to have and that **sentient beings** instinctively and mistakenly believe in. *See also* **emptiness**

self-grasping. *See* **ignorance**

self-liberation. *See* **nirvana**

self-realization. *See* **nirvana**

sentient being. Any being still cycling in one of the six realms of **samsara**.

seven-limb practice. Prostration, offering, confession, rejoicing, requesting the **guru** to teach, beseeching the guru to live long, and dedication of merit; performed as part of every **sadhana**.

Shakyamuni Buddha (563–483 B.C.). The fourth of the one thousand founding **buddhas** of this present world age, Buddha was born a prince of the Shakya clan in northern India, renounced his kingdom, achieved **enlight-**

enment at the age of thirty-five, and then taught the paths to liberation and enlightenment until he passed away at the age of eighty.

Shantideva. Great eighth-century Indian **Mahayana** saint, author of the seminal text *Way of the Bodhisattva,* chapter nine of which explains **emptiness.**

shunyata (Skt.). Literally, **emptiness.**

single-pointed concentration. One of the two modes of **meditation.** A subtle level of awareness, beyond the sensory or gross conceptual, attained in meditation, in which the practitioner can remain effortlessly focused on the chosen object of meditation.

spiritual master. *See* **guru**

superstition. *See* **delusion**

sutra (Skt.). A discourse or text of Buddha's general **Hinayana** and **Mahayana** teachings. Also a synonym for **Sutrayana.** *See also* **tantra**

Sutrayana (Skt.). The teachings of the combined **Hinayana** and **Paramitayana** parts of the path to **enlightenment.**

tathagata (Skt.). One gone to thusness; epithet of a **buddha.**

tathagatahood. See **enlightenment.**

tantra (Skt.). A discourse or text of Buddha's esoteric teachings. Also a synonym for **Tantrayana.** *See also* **sutra**

Tantrayana (Skt.). Vajrayana; Mantrayana; secret mantra; the quick path. The advanced, esoteric teachings of the **Mahayana** path to enlightenment, successful practice of which leads a person to **enlightenment** very quickly.

Three Precious Jewels. **Buddha** (the teacher), **Dharma** (his teachings), and **Sangha** (spiritual community); the three objects of Buddhist **refuge.**

three principal aspects of the path. The main **realizations** to be gained on the **Sutrayana** path as prerequisites to the practice of **tantra,** namely **renunciation, bodhichitta,** and **emptiness.**

totality. *See* **emptiness**

tranquil liberation. *See* **nirvana**

Vairochana. *See* **five conquerors**

Vajrasattva practice. A tantric practice in which one visualizes the Buddha Vajrasattva and recites his hundred-syllable **mantra**, specifically used to purify negative **karma**.

Vajrayana (Skt.). *See* **Tantrayana**

virtuous friend. *See* **guru**

wheel of Dharma. *See* **Dharmachakra**

wisdom-being. In this practice, the meditational **deity Avalokiteshvara** visualized at the heart of the **guru**.

wrong conception. *See* **delusion**

yidam (Tib.). Literally, mind seal. *See also* **deity**

yoga (Skt.). Literally, to yoke. The spiritual discipline to which one yokes oneself in order to achieve **enlightenment.**

yoga method. *See* **sadhana**

yogi (Skt.). An accomplished male tantric meditator.

yogini (Skt.). An accomplished female tantric meditator.

Suggested Further Reading

Bokar Rinpoche. *Chenrezig Lord of Love: Principles and Methods of Deity Meditation.* San Francisco: Clear Point Press, 1991.

Gyatso, Geshe Jampa. *Everlasting Rain: Purification Practice in Tibetan Buddhism.* Edited by Joan Nicell. Boston: Wisdom Publications, 1996.

Gyatso, Tenzin, the Fourteenth Dalai Lama. *Deity Yoga: In Action and Performance Tantra.* Translated and edited by Jeffrey Hopkins. Ithaca: Snow Lion Publications, 1981.

———. *The Union of Bliss & Emptiness: A Commentary on the Lama Choepa Guru Yoga Practice.* Translated by Thupten Jinpa. Ithaca: Snow Lion Publications, 1988.

———. *The World of Tibetan Buddhism: An Overview of Its Philosophy and Practice.* Translated and edited by Geshe Thupten Jinpa. Boston: Wisdom Publications, 1995.

Gyatso, Tenzin, the Fourteenth Dalai Lama and Alexander Berzin. *The Gelug/Kagyü Tradition of Mahamudra.* Ithaca: Snow Lion Publications, 1997.

Kongtrul, Jamgön. *Creation and Completion: Essential Points of Tantric Meditation.* Translated and introduced by Sarah Harding. Commentary by Thrangu Rinpoche. Boston: Wisdom Publications, 2002.

Namgyal, Takpo Tashi. *Mahāmudrā: The Quintessence of Mind and Meditation.* Translated by Lobsang Lhalungpa. Boston: Shambhala Publications, 1986.

Khyentse Rinpoche, Dilgo. *Guru Yoga: According to the Preliminary Practice of Longchen Nyingtik.* Translated by Matthieu Ricard. Ithaca: Snow Lion Publications, 1999.

Yeshe, Lama Thubten. *The Bliss of Inner Fire: Heart Practice of the Six Yogas of Naropa.* Edited by Robina Courtin and Ailsa Cameron. Boston: Wisdom Publications, 1998.

————. *Introduction to Tantra: The Transformation of Desire.* Edited by Jonathan Landaw. Boston: Wisdom Publications, 1987, 2001.

————. *The Tantric Path of Purification: The Yoga Method of Heruka Vajrasattva.* Edited by Nicholas Ribush. Boston: Wisdom Publications, 1995.

Yeshe, Lama and Lama Zopa Rinpoche. *Wisdom Energy: Basic Buddhist Teachings.* Edited by Jonathan Landaw with Alexander Berzin. Boston: Wisdom Publications, 1976, 2000.

Zopa Rinpoche, Lama Thubten. *The Door to Satisfaction: The Heart Advice of a Tibetan Buddhist Master.* Boston: Wisdom Publications, 2001.

————. *Teachings from the Vajrasattva Retreat.* Edited by Ailsa Cameron and Nicholas Ribush. Weston MA: The Lama Yeshe Wisdom Archive, 2000.

————. *Transforming Problems into Happiness.* Boston: Wisdom Publications, 2001.

————. *Ultimate Healing: The Power of Compassion.* Edited by Ailsa Cameron. Boston: Wisdom Publications, 2001.

Teachings by Kyabje Zopa Rinpoche on mandala offerings and on *The Foundation of All Good Qualities* are available through the Lama Yeshe Wisdom Archive (www.lamayeshe.com).

Index

Also from Wisdom Publications

Introduction to Tantra
THE TRANSFORMATION OF DESIRE
Lama Yeshe
Introduction by Jonathan Landaw ~ Foreword by Philip Glass
192 pages, ISBN 0-86171-162-9, $16.95

Tantra—so often misunderstood—is presented as a practice leading to joy and self-discovery, with a vision of reality that is simple, clear, and relevant to our lives.

"The best introductory work on Tibetan Buddhist tantra available, readily accessible to Western students." —Professor Janet Gyatso, Hershey Chair of Buddhist Studies, Harvard University

The Bliss of Inner Fire
HEART PRACTICE OF THE SIX YOGAS OF NAROPA
Lama Yeshe
224 pages, ISBN 0-86171-136-X, $16.95

In this collection of his last major teachings, Lama Yeshe illuminates the advanced practices for Highest Yoga Tantra, inspiring his students to discover for themselves their own capacity for inexhaustible bliss.

Following Je Tsongkhapa's text, *Having the Three Convictions,* Lama Yeshe introduces the renowned Six Yogas of Naropa, focusing mainly on the first of these six, the practice of inner fire *(tummo).* Mastery of inner fire quickly brings the mind to its most refined and penetrating state—the experience of clear light, an extraordinarily powerful state of mind that is unequaled in its ability to directly realize ultimate reality.

Wisdom Energy: Basic Buddhist Teachings
25TH ANNIVERSARY EDITION
Lama Yeshe and Lama Zopa Rinpoche
160 pp., ISBN 0-86171-170-X, $14.95

In this warm and compelling volume, two renowned teachers of Tibetan Buddhism present an entire meditation course. With humor and clarity, Lama Yeshe and Lama Zopa help us to uncover and renounce causes of unhappiness, grasp the purpose of meditation, and realize the advantages of acting with enlightened motives in the interests of all beings. These teachings are simple and straightforward, yet they open the door to true realization.

"A wonderful book, filled with profound wisdom and useful advice. I highly recommend it."—Howard C. Cutler, M.D., co-author of *The Art of Happiness*

The Tantric Path of Purification
THE YOGA METHOD OF HERUKA VAJRASATTVA
Lama Yeshe ~ Compiled and edited by Nick Ribush
344 pages, ISBN 0-86171-020-7, $18.95

This powerful purification practice has proven to be especially effective for Western practitioners. Lama Yeshe cuts through misconceptions and explains this method in detail. Included is an entire section of complete retreat instructions—required reading for anyone undertaking a meditational retreat in the Tibetan tradition.

Transforming Problems Into Happiness
Lama Zopa Rinpoche
Foreword by the Dalai Lama
104 pp., ISBN 0-86171-194-7, $12.95

"This book takes on the revolutionary Buddhist perspective: problems can be a path to the end of suffering, and we can learn to enjoy them as we would a good piece of music. This book offers specific guidance and practices to do just that. This is a good book to read and reread; you don't forget it."—*Inquiring Mind*

Essence of the Heart Sutra
THE DALAI LAMA'S HEART OF WISDOM TEACHINGS
Tenzin Gyatso, the 14th Dalai Lama
192 pages, ISBN 0-86171-318-4, $22.95

Distilled from the Dalai Lama's famous Heart of Wisdom teachings of 2001, this is the best available resource for studying and understanding one of Buddhism's seminal and best-known texts. *The Heart Sutra* is a presentation of profound wisdom on the nature of emptiness and selflessness, but these terms can be easily misunderstood. Here, the Dalai Lama identifies misconceptions and shows how an understanding of emptiness leads not to nihilism, but to a view of reality and to a deep and compassionate understanding.

Reincarnation
THE BOY LAMA
Vicki Mackenzie
200 pages, ISBN 0-86171-108-4, $16.95

Osel Hita Torres became the focus of world attention when he was recognized by the Dalai Lama as the reincarnation of Lama Yeshe. This story tells of Lama Yeshe's life, death, and rebirth as the little Lama Osel, while explaining the controversial phenomenon of reincarnation in a clear, engaging, and practical way.

"A dazzling and inspiring adventure story."—Bernardo Bertolucci

Practicing the Path
A COMMENTARY ON THE LAMRIM CHENMO
Yangsi Rinpoche ~ Foreword by Geshe Lhundub Sopa
576 pages, ISBN 0-86171-346-X, $24.95

A complete commentary on the *Lamrim Chenmo* in a single volume. Yangsi Rinpoche, a young tulku with the full training of a Tibetan scholar, here demonstrates his ability to teach to the Western mind. Beautifully edited and enjoyable to read, this is an excellent resource for those meditating on the *lamrim,* the steps on the path to enlightenment.

Ultimate Healing

THE POWER OF COMPASSION

Lama Zopa Rinpoche ~ *Foreword by Lillian Too*

288 pages, ISBN 0-86171-195-5, $16.95

We experience illness on a physical level, but in order to be healed, we must understand where true healing begins: within our hearts and minds. In *Ultimate Healing*, Lama Zopa shows us that by opening up to the truths of impermanence, interdependence, and the suffering of others, we can heal our bodies, our lives, and the world around us.

"An excellent book for those who face illness or care for the sick. Zopa Rinpoche explains methods to transform the minds of self-pity and anger, to work creatively with adversity, and to make our lives meaningful, no matter what state of health we are in."—Thubten Chodron, author of *Buddhism for Beginners*

Peacock in the Poison Grove

TWO BUDDHIST TEXTS FOR TRAINING THE MIND

Geshe Lhundub Sopa

with Michael Sweet and Leonard Zwilling

320 pages, ISBN 0-86171-185-8, $19.95

Lama Yeshe's teacher offers insightful commentary on of the earliest Tibetan texts that focus on mental training.

"The two long poems translated here are among the oldest and most dramatic of the mind-training texts, woven as they are of startling imagery and a quintessentially Tibetan admixture of sutra and tantra practices. *Peacock in the Poison Grove* provides lucid translations of the texts, and a humane and learned commentary revealing why Geshe Sopa has long been regarded as one of the greatest living scholars of Tibetan Buddhism."—Professor Roger Jackson, Carleton College, author of *Is Enlightenment Possible?*

About Wisdom

W ISDOM PUBLICATIONS, a nonprofit publisher, is dedicated to making available authentic Buddhist works for the benefit of all. We publish translations of the sutras and tantras, commentaries and teachings of past and contemporary Buddhist masters, and original works by the world's leading Buddhist scholars. We publish our titles with the appreciation of Buddhism as a living philosophy and with the special commitment to preserve and transmit important works from all the major Buddhist traditions.

To learn more about Wisdom, or to browse books online, visit our website at wisdompubs.org.

You may request a copy of our mail-order catalog online or by writing to:

Wisdom Publications
199 Elm Street
Somerville, Massachusetts 02144 USA
Telephone: (617) 776-7416
Fax: (617) 776-7841
Email: info@wisdompubs.org
www.wisdompubs.org

THE WISDOM TRUST

As a nonprofit publisher, Wisdom is dedicated to the publication of fine Dharma books for the benefit of all sentient beings and dependent upon the kindness and generosity of sponsors in order to do so. If you would like to make a donation to Wisdom, please do so through our Somerville office. If you would like to sponsor the publication of a book, please write or email us at the address above.

Thank you.

Wisdom is a nonprofit, charitable 501(c)(3) organization affiliated with the Foundation for the Preservation of the Mahayana Tradition (FPMT).

The Foundation for the Preservation
of the Mahayana Tradition

The Foundation for the Preservation of the Mahayana Tradition (FPMT) is an international network of Buddhist centers and activities dedicated to the transmission of Mahayana Buddhism as a practiced and living tradition. The FPMT was founded in 1975 by Lama Thubten Yeshe and is now under the spiritual direction of Lama Thubten Zopa Rinpoche. It is composed of Dharma teaching centers, monasteries, retreat centers, publishing houses, healing centers, hospices, and projects for the construction of stupas, statues, and othe holy objects. To find out more about the FPMT, contact:

FPMT International Office
PO Box 888, Taos NM 87571 USA
(505) 758-7766 • www.fpmt.org

THE LAMA YESHE WISDOM ARCHIVE

The Lama Yeshe Wisdom Archive (LYWA) is the collected works of Lama Thubten Yeshe and Lama Thubten Zopa Rinpoche. The Archive was founded in 1996 by Kyabje Zopa Rinpoche, its spiritual director, to make available in various ways the teachings it contains. Distribution of free booklets of edited teachings is one of the ways.

The LYWA makes every effort to organize the transcription of those teachings not yet transcribed, to edit those teachings not yet edited, and to otherwise archive and make available the Dharma legacy of these two great teachers. For more information, please contact us at:

The Lama Yeshe Wisdom Archive
PO Box 356, Weston MA 02493 USA
(781) 899-9587 • www.lamayeshe.com

Advice from a Spiritual Friend
Geshe Rabten and Geshe Dhargyey
Introduction by Stephen Batchelor
176 pages, ISBN 0-86171-193-9, $15.95

Like wise old friends, two Tibetan masters offer down-to-earth advice for cultivating compassion, wisdom, and happiness in every situation. Based on practical Buddhist verses on "thought training," *Advice from a Spiritual Friend* teaches how to develop the inner skills that lead to contentment by responding to everyday difficulties with patience and joy.

"Reading this book is akin to taking a personal retreat with two kindly and wise teachers. The instructions for realizing compassion in everyday life are readable and clear, and offer enhanced spiritual skills to readers of any background and orientation."—*NAPRA ReVIEW*

Wheel of Great Compassion
THE PRACTICE OF THE PRAYER WHEEL IN TIBETAN BUDDHISM
Compiled and introduced by Lorne Ladner
Foreword by Lama Zopa Rinpoche
168 pages, ISBN 0-86171-174-2, $19.95

"Prayer wheels are a ubiquitous element of Tibetan Buddhist practice, yet, especially in the West, little has been previously known of their history and proper use. In this jewel of a book, Lorne Ladner has brought together important textual sources, a Lama Zopa discourse, and his own personal experience to describe the symbolism, proper construction, ritual, and benefits of prayer wheel practice."—Prof. Jan Willis, author of *Dreaming Me: An African American Woman's Spiritual Journey*